A Passion *for* Fresh

A Passion *for* Fresh

100 FRESH & TASTY RECIPES TO LOVE

Recipes by Linda Stephen

MACMILLAN CANADA
TORONTO

Canadian Cataloguing in Publication Data

Stephen, Linda, 1945-
    A passion for fresh

Includes index
ISBN 0-7715-7615-3

I. Cookery I. Title
TX714.S83 1998   641.5   C98-932581-4

1 2 3 4 5 WC 03 02 01 00 99

Macmillan Canada
A Division of Canada Publishing Corporation
Toronto, Ontario, Canada

Editing by Shelley Tanaka

Design and page composition by
Joseph Gisini /Andrew Smith Graphics Inc.

Photographs by Michael Kohn

Food styling by Olga Truchan, except for
Steak Teriyaki with Springtime Asparagus and
Caesar Corn Salad with Chèvre Crostini by Julie Aldis

Illustrations by Jun Park

AN ALPHA CORPORATION BOOK
Vice-President and Publisher, Susan Yates

Front cover photograph: Arugula Salad with Oranges (recipe, page 19)
Back cover photograph: Lemon Ricotta Strawberry Shortcake (recipe, page 116)

We acknowledge the financial support of the Government of Canada through the Book Publishing Industry Development Program for our publishing activities.

PRINTED AND BOUND IN CANADA

Contents

Introduction

Twenty-five years ago, I started my cooking school because I had
a passion for good food and good-quality ingredients. Over the years
my appreciation of people with the same values has grown stronger
and stronger. Longo's shares this vision.

We love shopping at Longo's. The produce is excellent, the prices
are fair and the staff is always so conscientious and friendly. Qualities
like these start at the top. Since they opened more than forty years
ago, the Longo family has been committed to high standards not only
in what they sell but in how they treat their customers and staff.
I think of Longo's as an urban supermarket with country market
feeling and values.

Linda Stephen, who has created the recipes for this book, has
worked with me in my school for twenty years, and her great taste
and knowledge of food are reflected in both her teaching and her
cooking. As one of my favourite guest chefs, John Ash, likes to say, the
job of a good cook is to buy the best-quality ingredients and then
don't mess them up. Linda is the perfect example of such a cook.

Linda's recipes will show you how to make the most of the
wonderful ingredients Longo's has to offer. Whether you're cooking
for family or friends, you can't go wrong with this book.

BONNIE STERN

Recipes

Appetizers and Salads

Goat Cheese and Olive Spread

Eggplant "Guacamole"

Thai-flavoured Stuffed Mushrooms

Spinach and Feta Phyllo Spirals

Mini Pizzas Margherita

Thai Noodle Salad

Fajita Salad

Arugula Salad with Oranges

Caesar Corn Salad with Chèvre Crostini

Chopped Bistro Salad with Herb Dressing

Savoy Cabbage Slaw with Prosciutto Dressing

Radicchio Endive Salad

Couscous Salad Niçoise

Goat Cheese and Olive Spread

4 oz	goat cheese (chèvre)	125 g
4 oz	cream cheese or ricotta cheese, at room temperature	125 g
2	green onions, chopped	2
¼ cup	chopped fresh basil	50 mL
2 tbsp	olive oil	25 mL
2 tbsp	lemon juice	25 mL
¼ cup	coarsely chopped black olives	50 mL
½ tsp	pepper	2 mL
	Assorted fresh vegetables (carrots, celery, fennel, green beans, cauliflower), cut in bite-sized pieces	

1. Blend together goat cheese and cream cheese in food processor or by hand until smooth.

2. Add green onions, basil, olive oil and lemon juice. Blend until smooth. Add olives and pepper and combine just to incorporate olives.

3. Spoon mixture into a serving dish. Serve with fresh vegetables.

Makes 6 to 8 servings
PREPARATION TIME: 12 minutes

Eggplant "Guacamole"

2	oriental eggplants (page 104) or 1 medium eggplant, cut in ½-inch/1 cm cubes	2
1 tbsp	olive oil	15 mL
¼ cup	finely diced red onion	50 mL
3	tomatoes, seeded and chopped	3
2 tbsp	lime juice	25 mL
2 tbsp	finely chopped fresh cilantro (page 39)	25 mL
1 tsp	finely chopped fresh ginger (page 46)	5 mL
½ tsp	sesame oil	2 mL
¼ tsp	salt	1 mL
	Cucumber slices or tortilla chips	

Sesame Oil

Sesame oil is generally used in small amounts as a flavouring, not as a cooking oil. The dark Asian variety is richer and more flavourful than the North American or European oils. Store the oil in the refrigerator once it has been opened.

1. In a large bowl, combine eggplant with olive oil. Place on a parchment-lined baking sheet. Cook in a preheated 400°F/200°C oven for 20 to 25 minutes or until eggplant is golden and tender. Remove and cool slightly.

2. Return eggplant to bowl and toss well with onion, tomatoes, lime juice, cilantro, ginger, sesame oil and salt.

3. Spoon mixture into a serving dish. Let stand for up to 3 hours. Serve with cucumber slices or tortilla chips.

Makes 6 servings
PREPARATION TIME: 10 minutes
COOKING TIME: 25 minutes

Thai-flavoured Stuffed Mushrooms

Hoisin Sauce

Hoisin sauce is a sweet, pungent, soy-based ingredient used in Asian sauces and marinades.

12 oz	ground chicken	375 g
1 tbsp	finely chopped fresh ginger (page 46)	15 mL
1	clove garlic, minced	1
4	green onions, chopped, divided	4
2 tbsp	finely chopped fresh cilantro (page 39)	25 mL
4 tbsp	soy sauce, divided	50 mL
2 tbsp	finely chopped peanuts (optional)	25 mL
1 tbsp	cornstarch	15 mL
24	large mushrooms, stems removed	24
½ cup	chicken stock	125 mL
2 tbsp	oyster sauce or hoisin sauce	25 mL
2 tbsp	lime juice	25 mL
1 tsp	granulated sugar	5 mL
2 tbsp	vegetable oil	25 mL

1. In a bowl, combine ground chicken, ginger, garlic, 1 green onion, cilantro, 2 tbsp/25 mL soy sauce, peanuts and cornstarch.

2. Divide mixture evenly and place in mushroom cavities.

3. To prepare sauce, in another bowl, combine chicken stock, oyster sauce, lime juice, remaining 2 tbsp/25 mL soy sauce, sugar and remaining 3 green onions. Reserve.

4. Heat oil in a large non-stick skillet on medium-high heat. Add mushrooms, filling side up. Cook for 4 minutes.

5. Add reserved sauce. Cover mushrooms and steam over medium heat for 15 minutes until chicken is cooked.

6. Remove mushrooms to a serving platter. Reduce juices in pan for 2 to 3 minutes or until syrupy. Pour over mushrooms. Serve hot.

Makes 24 mushrooms
PREPARATION TIME: 10 minutes
COOKING TIME: 25 minutes

Spinach and Feta Phyllo Spirals

1½ cups	ricotta cheese	375 mL
1 cup	crumbled feta cheese	250 mL
¼ tsp	grated nutmeg	1 mL
1 lb	fresh spinach, cooked, chopped and squeezed dry, or 10 oz/300 g frozen chopped spinach, defrosted and squeezed dry	500 g
¼ cup	chopped fresh dill (or 1 tbsp/15 mL dried)	50 mL
2	green onions, chopped	2
¼ tsp	salt	1 mL
¼ tsp	pepper	1 mL
¼ cup	butter, melted	50 mL
2 tbsp	water	25 mL
6	sheets phyllo pastry	6
½ cup	dry breadcrumbs	125 mL

1. In a mixing bowl, combine ricotta, feta and nutmeg. Stir in spinach, dill, green onions, salt and pepper.

2. In a small bowl, combine melted butter and water.

3. Place 1 sheet of phyllo pastry on a flat surface (keeping remaining pastry covered with tea towel). Brush pastry lightly with butter mixture. Sprinkle with 2 tbsp/25 mL breadcrumbs. Cover with second sheet of pastry and 2 tbsp/25 mL breadcrumbs. Top with third sheet of pastry.

4. Cover two-thirds of pastry with half of filling, all the way down long side. Brush remaining third with butter mixture. Roll up jelly-roll style starting from long filled edge.

5. Using a sharp serrated knife, cut into 18 to 20 pieces. Place spirals cut side down on parchment-lined baking sheet.

6. Repeat with remaining pastry and filling.

7. Bake spirals in a preheated 375°F/190°C oven for 15 to 20 minutes or until golden and crispy. Serve warm. (These can also be baked until light golden, about 12 minutes, cooled, packaged and frozen for up to 4 weeks. To heat, place frozen spirals on a baking sheet and heat in a preheated 350°F/180°C oven for 12 to 15 minutes or until heated through.)

Makes 36 to 40 spirals
PREPARATION TIME: 25 minutes
COOKING TIME: 20 minutes

Ricotta

Ricotta is a soft, unripened cow's milk cheese originally from Italy. It has a mild flavour similar to cottage cheese and a light, creamy consistency. It is used in lasagna, cannelloni, spreads and desserts.

Goat Cheese

Feta is a white, unripened cheese made from goat's or sheep's milk. It is sold in blocks, either prepackaged or stored in brine. It can be crumbled or diced and is often used in salads. Chèvre is a creamy, mild cheese also made from goat's milk. Although feta is of Greek origin and chèvre of French origin, good-quality versions of both are made in Canada. The two cheeses are interchangeable in some recipes, but the texture is quite different, and feta usually has a sharper taste than chèvre.

Mini Pizzas Margherita

6	6-inch/15 cm flour tortillas	6
¾ cup	grated mozzarella cheese	175 mL
1 cup	thick tomato sauce	250 mL
⅓ cup	storebought or homemade basil pesto	75 mL
24	whole fresh basil leaves	24
¼ cup	grated Parmesan cheese	50 mL
2 tbsp	olive oil	25 mL

1. Arrange tortillas on baking sheets. Sprinkle evenly with mozzarella, leaving a ½-inch/1 cm border.

2. Spoon tomato sauce at intervals over cheese. Dot surface with pesto. Arrange basil leaves over top. Sprinkle with Parmesan and drizzle with olive oil.

3. Bake in a preheated 375°F/190°C oven for 12 minutes until cheese has melted and edges are just starting to colour.

4. Cool pizzas for 5 minutes. Cut each into 4 or 6 pieces. Serve hot or warm.

Makes 24 to 36 pieces
PREPARATION TIME: 10 minutes
COOKING TIME: 12 minutes

Thai Noodle Salad

8 oz	thin rice noodles	250 g
2	carrots, grated	2
½	English cucumber, halved, seeded and thinly sliced	½
6	radishes, thinly sliced	6
2	green onions, chopped	2
¼ cup	chopped fresh mint	50 mL
¼ cup	chopped fresh cilantro (page 39)	50 mL
½ cup	lime juice	125 mL
1 tbsp	soy sauce	15 mL
2 tbsp	granulated sugar	25 mL
1 tsp	finely chopped fresh ginger (page 46)	5 mL
½ tsp	hot red pepper sauce (optional)	2 mL
½ tsp	sesame oil (page 13)	2 mL
1 cup	sweet red pepper strips	250 mL

Lemons and Limes

Use freshly squeezed lime juice or lemon juice if you can — the flavour is superior to the bottled juices. If a recipe calls for lemon or lime rind, wash the fruit first, and dry it well. Grate it with a hand grater or zester, being careful not to include too much of the bitter white pith.

1. Drop noodles into boiling water for 2 minutes until just softened. Drain and rinse well with cold water.

2. Cut noodles into 4-inch/10 cm lengths with scissors and place in a salad bowl. Combine with carrots, cucumber, radishes, green onions, mint and cilantro.

3. To prepare dressing, in a bowl, whisk together lime juice, soy sauce, sugar, ginger, red pepper sauce and sesame oil.

4. Pour dressing over salad. Toss well and let marinate for 1 hour. Garnish with pepper strips. Serve cold or at room temperature.

Makes 6 servings
PREPARATION TIME: 20 to 25 minutes

Fajita Salad

Tortillas

Tortillas are thin flatbreads. Wheat-based tortillas are sometimes called flour tortillas and are often used in quesadillas, rollups or as a pizza base. Traditionally, corn tortillas are used in Mexican dishes such as tacos and burritos.

To warm tortillas, grill lightly on both sides or wrap in foil and heat in a preheated 300°F/150°C oven for 10 minutes.

2 tbsp	lime juice	25 mL
2 tbsp	olive oil	25 mL
2 tbsp	Dijon mustard	25 mL
½ tsp	pepper	2 mL
2	striploin steaks (total weight 12 oz/375 g)	2
4	tomatoes, diced	4
1	avocado, diced	1
½	red onion, cut in thin strips	½
1	sweet green pepper, seeded and diced	1
⅓ cup	chopped fresh cilantro (page 39)	75 mL
3 tbsp	lime juice	45 mL
3 tbsp	olive oil	45 mL
½ tsp	salt	2 mL
¼ tsp	pepper	1 mL
8	leaves Romaine lettuce, shredded	8
1 cup	grated Monterey Jack cheese	250 mL
6	10-inch/25 cm flour tortillas, warmed	6

1. In a small bowl, whisk together lime juice, oil, mustard and pepper. Rub into steak. Marinate steak, refrigerated, for 1 to 3 hours.

2. Preheat barbecue and brush with oil. Cook steak for 3 to 4 minutes per side or until medium. Remove from heat and let stand for 5 minutes. (Alternatively, cook steaks under a preheated broiler for 4 minutes per side.)

3. In a mixing bowl, combine tomatoes, avocado, onion, green pepper and cilantro. Add lime juice, oil, salt and pepper. Toss gently.

4. Arrange lettuce in a large serving bowl. Spoon tomato mixture over lettuce.

5. Carve steak diagonally into thin slices. Arrange over salad. Top with cheese. Serve salad with tortillas.

Makes 6 servings
PREPARATION TIME: 15 minutes plus marinating time
COOKING TIME: 10 minutes plus standing time

Arugula Salad
with Oranges

2	bunches arugula	2
5	oranges	5
2 tbsp	olive oil	25 mL
2 tbsp	red wine vinegar	25 mL
¼ tsp	salt	1 mL
¼ tsp	pepper	1 mL
¼ cup	pine nuts or walnuts, toasted (page 27)	50 mL
⅓ cup	chopped red onion	75 mL

Arugula

Arugula is a peppery green that can be used both in cooked dishes and in salads. Wash it well to remove any sand before using.

1. Break arugula into pieces and place in a salad bowl.

2. Peel oranges and cut into sections, reserving juices.

3. In a small bowl, whisk together oil, vinegar, reserved juices, salt and pepper.

4. To serve, add oranges, nuts, red onion and dressing to arugula. Toss lightly before serving.

Makes 6 servings
PREPARATION TIME: 10 minutes

Caesar Corn Salad with Chèvre Crostini

Sun-dried Tomatoes

Sun-dried tomatoes are full of concentrated flavour, and they add a savoury sweetness to salads and other dishes. They are sold dry-packed or oil-packed. To rehydrate the dry-packed tomatoes, sprinkle with a little water and warm briefly in the microwave. Use the oil from oil-packed tomatoes in salad dressings or on pizzas.

12	slices thin French bread (½ inch/1 cm thick)	12
1¼ cups	crumbled goat cheese (chèvre)	300 mL
1 tbsp	olive oil	15 mL
2 tbsp	chopped sun-dried tomatoes	25 mL
1	clove garlic, minced	1
2 tbsp	chopped fresh basil	25 mL
¼ tsp	pepper	1 mL
1	head Romaine lettuce, broken in bite-sized pieces (10 cups/2.5 L)	1
1½ cups	corn niblets, fresh (page 34) or frozen and defrosted	375 mL
½ cup	grated Parmesan cheese	125 mL
⅓ cup	pine nuts, toasted (page 27)	75 mL
2 tbsp	chopped fresh chives	25 mL
½ cup	storebought or homemade Caesar salad dressing	125 mL
	Whole chives for garnish	

1. To prepare crostini, place bread slices on a baking sheet and toast lightly in a preheated 350°F/180°C oven for 3 to 4 minutes per side. Cool.

2. In a small bowl, combine goat cheese with oil. Blend in sun-dried tomatoes, garlic, basil and pepper.

3. Place lettuce, corn, Parmesan, pine nuts and chopped chives in a large bowl. Add Caesar salad dressing and toss well.

4. Arrange salad on serving dishes. Spread toast slices with goat cheese. Top salad with crostini. Garnish with whole chives.

Makes 6 servings
PREPARATION TIME: 15 minutes
COOKING TIME: 8 minutes

Chopped Bistro Salad with Herb Dressing

1	small bunch broccoli	1
1	sweet red or yellow pepper, seeded and diced	1
1	carrot, peeled and grated	1
½	English cucumber, seeded and diced	½
2	stalks celery, coarsely chopped	2
1	clove garlic, minced	1
2 tbsp	chopped fresh parsley	25 mL
2 tbsp	chopped fresh chives or green onion	25 mL
1 tbsp	chopped fresh dill	15 mL
2 tbsp	lemon juice	25 mL
2 tbsp	red wine vinegar	25 mL
⅓ cup	olive oil	75 mL
¼ tsp	salt	1 mL
¼ tsp	pepper	1 mL

1. Break broccoli florets into small pieces. Peel stems and cut into small pieces.

2. In a large bowl, combine broccoli, sweet pepper, carrot, cucumber and celery.

3. In a small bowl, combine garlic, parsley, chives, dill, lemon juice, vinegar, olive oil, salt and pepper. Whisk to combine well.

4. Pour dressing over salad ingredients. Toss well and serve.

Makes 6 servings
PREPARATION TIME: 20 minutes

Savoy Cabbage Slaw with Prosciutto Dressing

¼ cup	olive oil	50 mL
8	thin slices prosciutto, diced	8
2	shallots, chopped	2
¼ cup	cider vinegar	50 mL
1 tbsp	liquid honey	15 mL
2 tbsp	chopped fresh parsley	25 mL
¼ tsp	pepper	1 mL
4 cups	thinly sliced Savoy cabbage	1 L
1	carrot, peeled and grated	1
2	green onions, chopped	2

Cabbage

Cabbage is one of the few green vegetables locally available almost year round, though it is at its peak in September and October. Red cabbage is a good accompaniment for pork and chicken. The Savoy and nappa varieties are good in salads; bok choy works well in stir-fries.

To slice cabbage, remove any tough or discoloured outer leaves. Cut the head into quarters and remove the core. Slice each quarter lengthwise into thin shreds.

Cabbage should be stored in the refrigerator for up to two weeks.

1. Heat olive oil in a skillet over medium heat. Add prosciutto and cook for 2 minutes until shrivelled. Add shallots and cook for 1 minute.

2. Remove pan from heat. Stir in vinegar, honey, parsley and pepper.

3. Place cabbage, carrot and green onions in a serving bowl. Add dressing from skillet and toss well.

Makes 6 servings
PREPARATION TIME: 25 minutes

Radicchio Endive Salad

2	Belgian endive	2
2	heads radicchio, shredded	2
1	bunch arugula, broken in pieces (page 19)	1
1	sweet red pepper, seeded and cut in strips	1
1	sweet yellow pepper, seeded and cut in strips	1
1	6-oz/170 mL jar marinated artichoke hearts, drained and halved	1
¼ cup	grated Parmesan cheese	50 mL
2 tsp	coarse-grain mustard	10 mL
2 tbsp	red wine vinegar	25 mL
2 tbsp	balsamic vinegar	25 mL
⅓ cup	olive oil	75 mL
¼ tsp	salt	1 mL
¼ tsp	pepper	1 mL

1. Separate endive leaves and cut into thin strips. Arrange endive, radicchio, arugula, sweet pepper strips, artichokes and cheese in a serving bowl.

2. To prepare dressing, in a small bowl, whisk together mustard, both vinegars, oil, salt and pepper. Pour over salad. Toss and serve.

Makes 6 servings
PREPARATION TIME: 20 minutes

Radicchio

Look for small, round, tightly packed heads of radicchio. The bright-red and white leaves add colour and a tart, slightly bitter taste to salads and cole slaws.

Belgian Endive

Belgian endive heads are elongated and tightly packed. The pale-yellow leaves have a sharp flavour and can be used raw or cooked. To slice for salads, cut off the base, separate the leaves and slice thinly crosswise or lengthwise.

Couscous Salad Niçoise

¼ cup	lemon juice	50 mL
¼ cup	olive oil	50 mL
¾ tsp	salt, divided	3 mL
¼ tsp	pepper	1 mL
1 cup	couscous	250 mL
¼ tsp	ground cumin	1 mL
1 cup	boiling water	250 mL
8 oz	green beans, cooked and cut in thirds	250 g
1	6-oz/170 mL jar marinated artichoke hearts, halved, with juices	1
1	6½-oz/184 g can tuna, drained and broken in chunks	1
¼ cup	chopped red onion	50 mL
1 tbsp	capers (page 31)	15 mL
3	anchovies, rinsed and diced (optional)	3
1	head radicchio, shredded (page 23)	1
¼ cup	black or green olives, pitted	50 mL
3	tomatoes, cut in wedges	3
	Fresh parsley leaves	

1. To prepare dressing, in a small bowl, combine lemon juice, olive oil, ½ tsp/2 mL salt and pepper. Reserve.

2. Place couscous, cumin and remaining ¼ tsp/1 mL salt in a square 8-inch/2 L baking dish. Pour in boiling water. Cover dish with foil and let stand for 15 minutes. Fluff couscous with a fork. Cool slightly.

3. In a large mixing bowl, combine couscous, beans, artichoke hearts and juices, tuna, red onion, capers and anchovies. Add dressing and toss to combine. Taste and adjust seasonings.

4. Arrange radicchio on individual serving dishes or platter. Spoon salad over lettuce. Garnish with olives, tomato wedges and parsley leaves.

Makes 6 servings
PREPARATION TIME: 30 minutes

Fish and Poultry

Sweet and Sour Salmon Fillets

Roasted Salmon with Dill Pesto

Grilled Salmon with Mango Sauce

Sea Bass with Hoisin Sauce

Halibut with Cornmeal Herb Crust

Pan-fried Trout with Tomatoes,
Lemon and Capers

Roasted Chicken with Vegetable Herb Stuffing

Baked Chicken Breasts Dijon

Southwestern Grilled Chicken Breasts
with Corn Salsa

Rolled Chicken Breasts with Prosciutto
and Fontina

Stir-fried Chicken with Peanut Sauce

Chicken Bombay

Chicken with Provençal Flavours

Chicken and Black Bean Chili

Turkey Rolls with Apple Stuffing

Turkey Scallopini with Mushrooms and Marsala

Sweet and Sour Salmon Fillets

½ cup	chicken stock or vegetable stock	125 mL
⅓ cup	ketchup	75 mL
¼ cup	white vinegar	50 mL
2 tbsp	brown sugar	25 mL
2 tbsp	soy sauce	25 mL
1 tbsp	finely chopped fresh ginger (page 46)	15 mL
½ tsp	sesame oil (page 13)	2 mL
1 tbsp	cornstarch	15 mL
2 tsp	olive oil	10 mL
4	6-oz/175 g salmon fillets, ¾ inch/2 cm thick, skin removed	4
½ cup	grated carrot	125 mL
2	green onions, sliced diagonally	2

Salmon

Salmon is a rich-tasting saltwater fish that comes from both the Atlantic and Pacific coasts. The Pacific varieties (sockeye, coho, chum, pink and chinook) range in colour from bright coral (sockeye) to almost white (chinook). Atlantic salmon can be used in place of trout, arctic char or other mild-flavoured fish. Fresh or frozen salmon is mostly sold as steaks or fillets. It can be poached, steamed, grilled, pan-fried or baked.

1. In a small saucepan, combine stock, ketchup, vinegar, sugar, soy sauce, ginger, sesame oil and cornstarch. Place over medium heat and bring to a boil. Cook, stirring, for 1 minute until thickened. Reserve and keep warm.

2. Heat oil in a large non-stick skillet over medium-high heat. Pat salmon dry. Add salmon to pan and cook for 4 minutes per side.

3. Arrange salmon on serving dish. Spoon sauce over salmon. Garnish with carrot and green onions.

Makes 4 servings
PREPARATION TIME: 5 minutes
COOKING TIME: 12 minutes

Roasted Salmon
with Dill Pesto

2	green onions, chopped	2
1	clove garlic, minced	1
1 cup	fresh dill sprigs	250 mL
¾ cup	fresh parsley sprigs	175 mL
⅓ cup	pine nuts or almonds, toasted	75 mL
⅓ cup	olive oil	75 mL
2 tbsp	lemon juice	25 mL
½ tsp	salt	2 mL
¼ tsp	pepper	1 mL
4	6-oz/175 g salmon fillets, ¾ inch/2 cm thick, skin removed	4
	Fresh dill sprigs	
	Lemon wedges	

Toasting Nuts

To toast chopped or whole nuts, spread them on an ungreased baking sheet and bake in a preheated 300°F/150°C oven for 8 to 10 minutes, or until golden. Stir occasionally. Nuts can also be toasted on the stovetop in a dry skillet, but stir or shake the pan constantly and watch carefully, as they can burn quickly.

1. To prepare pesto, in a food processor or blender, combine onions, garlic, dill, parsley, nuts, oil, lemon juice, salt and pepper. Blend until smooth.

2. Rub pesto over both sides of salmon. Marinate, refrigerated, for 20 minutes.

3. Place salmon on a parchment-lined baking sheet. Roast in a preheated 425°F/210°C oven for 10 minutes until just cooked through.

4. Arrange salmon on serving dishes. Spoon over any pesto remaining on baking sheet. Garnish with dill sprigs and lemon wedges.

Makes 4 servings
PREPARATION TIME: 5 minutes plus 20 minutes marinating time
COOKING TIME: 10 minutes

Grilled Salmon with Mango Sauce

2 tbsp	lime juice	25 mL
1 tbsp	finely chopped fresh ginger (page 46)	15 mL
1 tbsp	olive oil	15 mL
4	6-oz/175 g salmon steaks, 1 inch/2.5 cm thick	4

MANGO SAUCE:

2	ripe mangoes, diced	2
2	green onions, chopped	2
2 tsp	chopped jalapeño pepper	10 mL
2 tbsp	olive oil	25 mL
2 tbsp	lime juice	25 mL
1 tsp	liquid honey	5 mL
¼ tsp	salt	1 mL
2 tbsp	chopped fresh cilantro (page 39)	25 mL

1. In a small bowl, combine lime juice, ginger and oil. Pour over salmon steaks and marinate, refrigerated, for 15 minutes.

2. To prepare sauce, in a mixing bowl, combine mangoes, green onions, jalapeño, oil, lime juice, honey, salt and cilantro. Stir to combine.

3. Heat grill pan, barbecue or broiler and brush lightly with oil. Add salmon steaks and cook for 4 to 5 minutes per side or until cooked through. Turn steaks carefully.

4. Serve salmon with mango sauce.

Makes 4 servings
PREPARATION TIME: 12 minutes plus 15 minutes marinating time
COOKING TIME: 10 minutes

Mangoes

Mangoes have an exotic, tropical flavour that can range from peach to banana. They are ripe when they yield slightly to pressure, and should be used within a day or so after they are ripe. Do not store them in the refrigerator as this alters the texture slightly.

Peel the fruit over a bowl to catch all the juice. Cut through on either side of the seed and dice these two large pieces, then cut away the pulp remaining around the seed.

Sea Bass with Hoisin Sauce

¼ cup	hoisin sauce (page 14)	50 mL
2 tbsp	orange juice concentrate	25 mL
2 tbsp	lemon juice	25 mL
2 tsp	finely chopped fresh ginger (page 46)	10 mL
½ tsp	sesame oil (page 13)	2 mL
4	6-oz/175 g boneless sea bass fillets or swordfish steaks, ¾ inch/2 cm thick, skin removed	4
1	tomato, cut in sections	1
2	green onions, sliced diagonally	2

1. In a small bowl, combine hoisin sauce, orange juice concentrate, lemon juice, ginger and oil. Stir well.

2. Place fish in a single layer in a shallow baking dish. Pour sauce over and turn fish several times to coat thoroughly.

3. Cover baking dish with foil. Bake in a preheated 400°F/200°C oven for 10 to 12 minutes or until fish just turns opaque.

4. Serve fish garnished with tomato sections and green onions.

Makes 4 servings
PREPARATION TIME: 5 minutes
COOKING TIME: 12 minutes

Halibut with Cornmeal Herb Crust

¾ cup	cornmeal	175 mL
1 tsp	dried oregano	5 mL
¼ tsp	ground cumin	1 mL
½ tsp	salt	2 mL
¼ tsp	pepper	1 mL
¾ cup	buttermilk or unflavoured yogurt	175 mL
4	6-oz/175 g halibut steaks, 1 inch/2.5 cm thick	4
2 tbsp	olive oil	25 mL
4	orange sections	4

Cooking Fish

Regardless of the cooking method, fresh fish should be cooked at high heat (400 to 425°F/200 to 220°C) for 10 minutes per inch of thickness (when the piece of fish is measured at its thickest point). To test for doneness, insert a fork or the tip of a sharp knife into the thickest part. The flesh inside should be opaque and just beginning to flake easily.

1. In a shallow dish, combine cornmeal, oregano, cumin, salt and pepper.

2. Pour buttermilk into a separate shallow dish.

3. Pat halibut steaks dry. Dip into buttermilk, draining off excess. Place in cornmeal mixture and turn to coat evenly.

4. Heat oil in an ovenproof non-stick skillet over medium-high heat. Add steaks and cook for 2 minutes per side, turning carefully.

5. Place pan in a preheated 400°F/200°C oven and cook fish for 10 to 12 minutes or until opaque in centre. Serve garnished with orange sections.

Makes 4 servings
PREPARATION TIME: 10 minutes
COOKING TIME: 15 minutes

Pan-fried Trout with Tomatoes, Lemon and Capers

2 tbsp	olive oil	25 mL
4	5-oz/150 g boneless trout fillets	4
	Salt and pepper to taste	
½ cup	white wine or chicken stock	125 mL
3	tomatoes, chopped	3
1	lemon, peeled and cut in ¼-inch/5 mm dice	1
2 tbsp	capers	25 mL
1 tbsp	chopped fresh tarragon or parsley	15 mL

Capers

Capers are the pickled buds and young berries of a prickly shrub that grows in Mediterranean countries. They are often used in fish dishes and salads. Drain and rinse them before using.

1. Heat oil in a large non-stick skillet on high heat. Pat trout dry and season with salt and pepper. Cook trout for 2 to 3 minutes per side or until golden. Remove to serving platter and keep warm.

2. Return skillet to heat. Pour in wine. Cook for 2 minutes. Add tomatoes, lemon and capers. Cook for 2 more minutes. Stir in tarragon.

3. Pour sauce over trout and serve.

Makes 4 servings
PREPARATION TIME: 5 minutes
COOKING TIME: 12 minutes

Roasted Chicken with Vegetable Herb Stuffing

Garlic

Not only an essential ingredient for most cooks, garlic is also eaten for its health benefits. Look for heads with plump cloves; avoid any that have sprouted. Peel the individual cloves and mince them through a garlic press if you are adding them to salad dressings. If you are sautéing the garlic, chop it finely with a knife, since the juices released with mincing cause it to burn more easily (if you do burn garlic, discard it and start again, as it will be very bitter).

Garlic becomes milder and sweeter the longer it is cooked. Add whole peeled cloves to the pan when you are roasting vegetables, or boil a few cloves with potatoes before mashing.

VEGETABLE HERB STUFFING:

1	onion, peeled and cut in ½-inch/1 cm pieces	1
2	carrots, peeled and cut in ½-inch/1 cm pieces	2
1	bulb fennel, trimmed and cut in ½-inch/1 cm pieces (page 106)	1
3	whole cloves garlic, peeled	3
3	sprigs fresh rosemary	3
1	sprig fresh sage	1
2 tbsp	lemon juice	25 mL
1 tbsp	olive oil	15 mL
¼ tsp	salt	1 mL
¼ tsp	pepper	1 mL
1	3-lb/1.5 kg chicken	1
	Olive oil	
	Coarse salt	
	Paprika	

1. In a mixing bowl, combine onion, carrots, fennel, garlic, rosemary, sage, lemon juice, oil, salt and pepper.

2. Pat chicken dry. Stuff with vegetable mixture. Close cavity and secure with metal skewers and kitchen twine.

3. Place chicken in a roasting pan. Brush with olive oil. Sprinkle with coarse salt and paprika. Roast in a preheated 400°F/200°C oven for 1½ hours until juices run clear at thigh when pierced with a sharp knife.

4. To serve, remove vegetable stuffing. Carve chicken and serve with stuffing.

Makes 6 servings
PREPARATION TIME: 15 minutes
COOKING TIME: 1½ hours

Photo (opposite):
Spinach and Feta
Phyllo Spirals
(see recipe page 15)

Photo (overleaf):
Arugula Salad
with Oranges
(see recipe page 19)

Baked Chicken Breasts Dijon

1¼ cups	fresh breadcrumbs	300 mL
½ cup	grated Parmesan cheese	125 mL
¼ cup	chopped fresh parsley	50 mL
2	cloves garlic, minced	2
1 tbsp	olive oil	15 mL
½ tsp	salt	2 mL
¼ tsp	pepper	1 mL
¼ cup	Dijon mustard	50 mL
6	boneless single chicken breasts, skin removed	6

1. In a mixing bowl, combine breadcrumbs, cheese, parsley, garlic, oil, salt and pepper.

2. Place chicken breasts on a parchment-lined baking sheet. Brush with mustard. Sprinkle crumb topping over mustard. Press so crumbs adhere to mustard.

3. Bake in a preheated 375°F/190°C oven for 25 minutes until chicken is cooked through.

Makes 6 servings
PREPARATION TIME: 12 minutes
COOKING TIME: 25 minutes

Photo (overleaf):
Grilled Salmon with
Mango Sauce
(see recipe page 28)

Photo (opposite):
Stir-fried Chicken
with Peanut Sauce
(see recipe page 36)

Southwestern Grilled Chicken Breasts with Corn Salsa

Fresh Corn

Look for fresh-looking silk and smallish kernels. Use corn as soon as possible after buying it, and do not remove the husks until just before cooking. To remove kernels from the cob, stand the cob upright in a shallow dish and cut off the kernels using a sawing motion — 3 cobs will yield about 1 ½ cups/375 mL niblets.

CORN SALSA:

1½ cups	corn niblets, fresh or frozen and defrosted	375 mL
2	tomatoes, diced	2
3	green onions, chopped	3
1	jalapeño pepper, seeded and chopped	1
¼ cup	chopped fresh cilantro (page 39)	50 mL
2 tbsp	orange juice concentrate	25 mL
2 tbsp	lime juice	25 mL
2 tbsp	olive oil	25 mL
	Salt and pepper to taste	

2 tsp	chili powder	10 mL
1 tsp	ground cumin	5 mL
1 tsp	dried oregano	5 mL
½ tsp	salt	2 mL
¼ tsp	pepper	1 mL
2	cloves garlic, minced	2
1 tbsp	olive oil	15 mL
6	boneless single chicken breasts, skin removed, flattened (page 35)	6

1. To prepare salsa, in a mixing bowl, combine corn, tomatoes, green onions, jalapeño, cilantro, orange juice concentrate, lime juice and olive oil. Season to taste with salt and pepper. Reserve.

2. To prepare chicken, in a small bowl, combine chili powder, cumin, oregano, salt, pepper, garlic and oil. Rub over chicken breasts.

3. Heat grill pan, barbecue or broiler and brush with oil. Cook chicken breasts for 3 minutes per side until just cooked through. (Alternatively, heat 1 tbsp/15 mL oil in a heavy non-stick skillet and cook chicken breasts.)

4. Serve chicken breasts with corn salsa.

Makes 6 servings
PREPARATION TIME: 15 minutes
COOKING TIME: 6 minutes

Rolled Chicken Breasts
with Prosciutto and Fontina

6	boneless single chicken breasts, skin removed, flattened	6
¼ tsp	salt	1 mL
¼ tsp	pepper	1 mL
½ tsp	dried oregano	2 mL
¼ tsp	paprika	1 mL
6	thin slices Fontina cheese	6
6	thin slices prosciutto	6
2 tbsp	olive oil, divided	25 mL
⅓ cup	chopped shallots	75 mL
½ cup	chicken stock	125 mL
¼ cup	whipping cream (optional)	50 mL
2 tbsp	lemon juice	25 mL
¼ cup	chopped fresh parsley	50 mL
6	lemon slices	6

Flattening Chicken Breasts

To flatten chicken breasts or veal or turkey scallopini, place the meat between two sheets of waxed paper or parchment. Using a meat pounder, rolling pin or the bottom of a heavy pot, pound gently to flatten, being careful not to tear the meat.

1. Season inside part of chicken breasts with salt, pepper, oregano and paprika. Arrange a slice of Fontina and prosciutto over each breast.

2. Roll up each chicken breast starting from smaller end. Secure with a small metal skewer or round toothpick.

3. Heat 1 tbsp/15 mL olive oil in a non-stick skillet on medium-high heat. Brown rolled chicken on all sides, about 4 minutes. Transfer to a shallow baking dish.

4. Heat remaining 1 tbsp/15 mL oil in pan. Add shallots and cook for 1 minute until softened. Stir in chicken stock, whipping cream and lemon juice. Reduce juices over high heat for 3 minutes until syrupy. Adjust seasonings to taste.

5. Pour sauce over chicken. Bake in a preheated 350°F/180°C oven for 25 minutes. Garnish each serving with parsley and a lemon slice.

Makes 6 servings
PREPARATION TIME: 12 minutes
COOKING TIME: 35 minutes

Stir-fried Chicken with Peanut Sauce

1½ lb	boneless chicken breasts, skin removed, cut in 1-inch/2.5 cm pieces	750 g
1 tsp	sesame oil (page 13)	5 mL
2 tsp	soy sauce	10 mL
2 tbsp	vegetable oil, divided	25 mL
3	cloves garlic, finely chopped	3
1 tbsp	finely chopped fresh ginger (page 46)	15 mL
3	green onions, chopped	3
1	sweet red pepper, seeded and cut in 1-inch/2.5 cm pieces	1
4 oz	green beans, diced	125 g
4 oz	snow peas, trimmed	125 g
½ cup	homemade (page 63) or storebought peanut sauce	125 mL
¼ cup	chopped fresh cilantro (page 39)	50 mL

1. Place chicken in a bowl and stir in sesame oil and soy sauce.

2. Heat 1 tbsp/15 mL vegetable oil in a wok or non-stick skillet on high heat. Add chicken and stir-fry for 2 to 3 minutes or until pinkness disappears. Remove chicken and set aside. Wipe out pan.

3. Heat remaining 1 tbsp/15 mL oil in wok or skillet. Add garlic, ginger and green onions. Stir-fry for 30 seconds. Add red pepper and beans. Stir-fry for 1 minute. Add peas and stir-fry for 1 minute.

4. Return chicken to pan. Stir in peanut sauce and cook until heated through. Sprinkle with cilantro. Serve with rice.

Makes 4 to 5 servings
PREPARATION TIME: 10 minutes
COOKING TIME: 10 minutes

Snow Peas

Snow peas, like sugar snaps, are edible podded peas. They are usually available year round but the local varieties are an early spring specialty. The freshest ones are shiny and bright green and they will squeak when two pods are rubbed together. To trim them, pull off the stem and pull down the length of the pod (on the side where the peas are attached) to remove the tough strings. The peas should be cooked only for a short time — just until tender but still crisp.

A PASSION FOR FRESH

Chicken Bombay

5	boneless single chicken breasts, skin removed	5
	Salt and pepper to taste	
2 tbsp	olive oil	25 mL
2	onions, thinly sliced	2
2	cloves garlic, thinly sliced	2
1 tbsp	finely chopped fresh ginger (page 46)	15 mL
2	red-skinned apples, cored and cut in 1-inch / 2.5 cm pieces	2
2 tsp	curry powder	10 mL
½ tsp	ground cumin	2 mL
½ tsp	salt	2 mL
¼ tsp	pepper	1 mL
½ cup	apple juice	125 mL
¼ cup	cider vinegar	50 mL
¼ cup	chopped fresh cilantro (page 39)	50 mL

Apples

Apple skins contain much of the flavour and nutritional value of the fruit, and red-skinned apples add colour and fibre to a dish. Apples do not need to be peeled for many dishes, including pies and crisps.

1. Cut chicken breasts thinly into 2-inch/5 cm strips. Pat dry and season lightly with salt and pepper.

2. Heat oil in a large skillet over medium-high heat. Add chicken pieces and cook for 3 to 4 minutes or until just cooked through. Remove from pan and keep warm.

3. Add onions, garlic, ginger and apples to skillet. Cook for 4 to 5 minutes or until softened. Add curry powder, cumin, salt and pepper. Cook for 1 minute.

4. Add apple juice and vinegar to skillet. Cover and cook for 3 to 4 minutes or until apples are tender. Stir in reserved chicken and heat through. Sprinkle with cilantro. Serve with rice or noodles.

Makes 6 servings
PREPARATION TIME: 10 minutes
COOKING TIME: 15 minutes

Chicken with Provençal Flavours

½ cup	all-purpose flour	125 mL
¼ tsp	salt	1 mL
¼ tsp	pepper	1 mL
12	chicken thighs or legs, skin removed	12
2 tbsp	olive oil	25 mL
2	onions, thinly sliced	2
12	whole cloves garlic, peeled	12
¼ tsp	hot red pepper flakes	1 mL
1 cup	chicken stock or dry white wine	250 mL
2	tomatoes, seeded and diced	2
2	medium zucchini, diced	2
1	eggplant (12 oz/375 g), diced	1
2 tsp	chopped fresh thyme (or ½ tsp/2 mL dried)	10 mL
½ cup	pitted black or green olives	125 mL
2 tbsp	chopped fresh parsley	25 mL

1. In a shallow dish, combine flour, salt and pepper. Coat chicken pieces in seasoned flour.

2. Heat oil in a large skillet over medium-high heat. In batches, cook chicken pieces on all sides for 6 to 8 minutes or until brown. Remove from skillet and reserve.

3. Add onions, garlic and hot pepper flakes to skillet. Cook for 6 to 8 minutes or until softened and golden. Add stock and loosen any brown bits on bottom of pan.

4. Add tomatoes, zucchini, eggplant and thyme to skillet. Bring to a boil. Add chicken pieces. Reduce heat. Cover and cook on medium-low heat for 35 minutes, stirring occasionally, until chicken is cooked.

5. Stir in olives and parsley.

Makes 6 to 8 servings
PREPARATION TIME: 15 minutes
COOKING TIME: 50 minutes

Chicken and Black Bean Chili

2 tbsp	olive oil	25 mL
1½ lb	ground chicken	750 g
2	onions, chopped	2
3	cloves garlic, finely chopped	3
1	sweet green pepper, seeded and diced	1
1 tbsp	chili powder	15 mL
1 tsp	ground cumin	5 mL
1 tsp	dried oregano	5 mL
1 tsp	salt	5 mL
½ tsp	pepper	2 mL
1½ cups	tomato juice	375 mL
2	tomatoes, chopped	2
1	19-oz/540 mL can black beans, drained and rinsed	1
2 cups	corn niblets, fresh (page 34) or frozen and defrosted	500 mL
⅓ cup	chopped fresh cilantro	75 mL
1 cup	grated Cheddar cheese	250 mL

Cilantro

Cilantro is the aromatic, leafy fresh herb that comes from the same plant as coriander seeds. It is also called fresh coriander or Chinese parsley. It adds a distinctive flavour to dishes, but fresh parsley can sometimes be used as a substitute.

1. Heat oil in a large saucepan on high heat. Add chicken and cook, stirring, for 4 minutes until pinkness disappears.

2. Add onions, garlic and green pepper to saucepan. Cook for 4 minutes until softened.

3. Add chili powder, cumin, oregano, salt, pepper, tomato juice, tomatoes and beans to saucepan. Bring to a boil. Reduce heat, cover and simmer for 30 minutes.

4. Stir in corn. Cook, uncovered, for 10 minutes. Serve sprinkled with cilantro and cheese.

Makes 8 to 10 servings
PREPARATION TIME: 15 minutes
COOKING TIME: 50 minutes

Turkey Rolls
with Apple Stuffing

APPLE STUFFING:

4 tbsp	olive oil, divided	50 mL
½	onion, chopped	½
1	apple, peeled, cored and diced	1
1½	slices stale bread, cut in cubes (1 cup/250 mL)	1½
½ tsp	dried sage or savory	2 mL
¼ cup	chicken stock or apple juice	50 mL
2 tbsp	chopped fresh parsley	25 mL
¼ tsp	salt	1 mL
¼ tsp	pepper	1 mL
8	pieces turkey scallopini, 5 x 3 inches/12.5 x 7.5 cm each	8
¼ cup	chicken stock or apple juice	50 mL
2 tbsp	chopped fresh parsley	25 mL

1. To prepare stuffing, heat 2 tbsp/25 mL oil in a large skillet on medium heat. Add onion and apple. Cook for 5 minutes until softened but not coloured. Place in a mixing bowl.

2. Add bread cubes, sage, stock, parsley, salt and pepper to mixing bowl. Combine and cool.

3. Place scallopini on a flat surface. Spread stuffing over scallopini leaving ½ inch/1 cm at one end. Roll scallopini and secure with skewers or toothpicks.

4. To cook, heat remaining 2 tbsp/25 mL oil in a large skillet over medium heat. Brown turkey rolls on all sides. Add stock. Cover and cook over medium-low heat for 10 minutes. Uncover and cook down juices for 5 minutes. Sprinkle with parsley.

Makes 4 to 6 servings
PREPARATION TIME: 20 minutes
COOKING TIME: 20 minutes

Turkey Scallopini with Mushrooms and Marsala

½ cup	all-purpose flour	125 mL
¼ tsp	salt	1 mL
¼ tsp	pepper	1 mL
1½ lb	turkey scallopini	750 g
2 tbsp	olive oil	25 mL
2	shallots, diced	2
8 oz	button mushrooms, sliced	250 g
½ tsp	dried tarragon	2 mL
½ cup	Marsala wine	125 mL
½ cup	whipping cream or chicken stock	125 mL
2 tbsp	chopped fresh parsley	25 mL

1. In a shallow dish, combine flour, salt and pepper. Pat turkey dry and dip each piece in seasoned flour. Shake off excess.

2. Heat oil in a large skillet over high heat. Cook scallopini for 1 minute per side until golden. (This may need to be done in batches, adding a small amount of oil if necessary.) Keep scallopini warm in a separate dish.

3. Reduce heat to medium-high. Add shallots to skillet and cook for 30 seconds. Add mushrooms and tarragon and cook for 2 minutes. Spoon mushrooms over turkey.

4. Pour Marsala and cream into skillet. Scrape bottom of pan to loosen any bits. Cook sauce for 4 minutes until slightly thickened.

5. Spoon sauce over turkey and mushrooms and sprinkle with parsley.

Makes 4 to 6 servings
PREPARATION TIME: 8 minutes
COOKING TIME: 15 minutes

Menus

Summer Barbecue

Goat Cheese and Olive
Spread with Fresh Vegetables
(page 12)

Steak Teriyaki (page 46)

Roasted Sweet Potatoes,
Onions and Cauliflower
(page 113)

Chopped Bistro Salad with
Herb Dressing (page 21)

Lemon Ricotta Strawberry
Shortcake (page 116)

Elegant Dinner

Thai-flavoured Stuffed
Mushrooms (page 14)

Herbed Leg of Lamb with
Roasted Sweet Potatoes
(page 53)

Zucchini with Tomato and
Oregano (page 112)

Arugula Salad with Oranges
(page 19)

Chocolate Raspberry Trifle
(page 122)

Meat

Shepherd's Pie with Sweet Potatoes and Corn

Old-fashioned Meatloaf

Steak Teriyaki

Beef and Pepper Paprikash

Roasted Beef Tenderloin with Mushroom Sauce

Beef and Vegetable Stir-fry

Veal Scallopini Piccata

Veal Chops with Cranberry Relish

Veal with Tomato Zucchini Sauce

Herbed Leg of Lamb with Roasted Sweet Potatoes

Grilled Lamb Chops with Jalapeño Mint Sauce

Sautéed Pork Chops with Apples

Stuffed Pork Tenderloin with Barbecue Glaze

Maple-glazed Ham Steaks with Pineapple

Shepherd's Pie with Sweet Potatoes and Corn

1 lb	sweet potatoes (2 large), peeled and cut in 2-inch/5 cm pieces	500 g
1 lb	potatoes (3 large), peeled and cut in 2-inch/5 cm pieces	500 g
½ cup	milk, warmed	125 mL
2 tbsp	butter	25 mL
¼ tsp	salt	1 mL
¼ tsp	pepper	1 mL
2 tbsp	olive oil	25 mL
1	onion, diced	1
2	cloves garlic, finely chopped	2
½ tsp	curry powder	2 mL
1 lb	lean ground beef	500 g
2 tbsp	all-purpose flour	25 mL
1 tbsp	Dijon mustard	15 mL
1 cup	beef stock or chicken stock	250 mL
½ tsp	salt	2 mL
¼ tsp	pepper	1 mL
¼ cup	chopped fresh parsley	50 mL
1½ cups	corn niblets, fresh or frozen and defrosted	375 mL

1. Cook sweet potatoes and potatoes in lightly salted boiling water for 20 minutes until tender. Drain well. Mash potatoes with warm milk, butter, salt and pepper. Reserve.

2. Meanwhile, heat oil in a large skillet over medium-high heat. Cook onion and garlic for 2 minutes until soft. Stir in curry powder. Cook for 30 seconds. Add beef and cook, stirring, until pinkness disappears, about 4 minutes. Drain off any fat.

3. Stir in flour and cook for 2 minutes. Mix in mustard, stock, salt and pepper. Cook for 4 minutes until mixture thickens. Adjust seasonings. Stir in parsley.

4. Spoon meat mixture into a lightly greased 10-cup/2.5 L shallow baking dish. Spread corn over meat. Spread potato mixture over corn. Bake in a preheated 375°F/190°C oven for 30 to 35 minutes or until bubbling at sides and top is slightly brown.

Makes 6 to 8 servings
PREPARATION TIME: 15 minutes
COOKING TIME: 70 minutes

Old-fashioned Meatloaf

1 tbsp	olive oil	15 mL
1	onion, chopped	1
½ cup	chopped celery	125 mL
½ cup	fresh breadcrumbs or rolled oats	125 mL
½ cup	grated Parmesan cheese	125 mL
⅓ cup	tomato juice or milk	75 mL
1	egg	1
8 oz	lean ground beef	250 g
8 oz	lean ground pork	250 g
½ tsp	dried savory or thyme	2 mL
½ tsp	salt	2 mL
¼ tsp	pepper	1 mL
½ cup	ketchup	125 mL

1. Heat oil in a small skillet over medium heat. Add onion and celery. Cook for 3 minutes until softened. Remove from heat and spoon into a large mixing bowl. Cool for 10 minutes.

2. To the cooked vegetables, add breadcrumbs, cheese, tomato juice, egg, beef, pork, savory, salt and pepper. Combine thoroughly.

3. Pat mixture into an 8-inch/2 L square baking dish. Spread with ketchup.

4. Bake in a preheated 350°F/180°C oven for 35 to 40 minutes or until a meat thermometer registers 160°F/70°C. To serve, cut into squares.

Makes 4 to 6 servings
PREPARATION TIME: 10 minutes
COOKING TIME: 40 minutes

Steak Teriyaki

½ cup	soy sauce	125 mL
½ cup	white wine or orange juice	125 mL
¼ cup	water	50 mL
⅓ cup	granulated sugar	75 mL
1	clove garlic, peeled and smashed	1
1	½-inch/1 cm piece fresh ginger root, smashed	1
1	2½-lb/1.25 kg sirloin steak, 1 inch/2.5 cm thick	1

Ginger Root

Fresh ginger adds a tangy, aromatic flavour to dishes and has a very different taste from powdered ginger. Look for smooth, plump roots without dry ends or mouldy patches. Peel it with a vegetable peeler. Leftovers can be frozen or covered with brandy and stored in the refrigerator.

1. Place soy sauce, wine, water, sugar, garlic and ginger in a saucepan. Bring to a boil. Reduce heat to medium and cook until liquid has reduced by half and is syrupy, about 15 minutes. Remove garlic and ginger. Cool sauce to room temperature.

2. Marinate steak in teriyaki sauce for 30 minutes, turning occasionally.

3. Remove steak from marinade and place on a preheated grill. Cook over medium-high heat for 8 minutes per side for medium-rare or until a meat thermometer registers 140°F/60°C. Remove steak from grill. Let stand for 10 minutes before carving into thin slices.

Makes 6 to 8 servings
PREPARATION TIME: 30 minutes for marinating
COOKING TIME: 20 minutes for sauce; 16 minutes for beef
plus standing time

Beef and Pepper Paprikash

1 lb	fast-fry striploin steaks (about 4 pieces), trimmed	500 g
2 tbsp	olive oil, divided	25 mL
2	onions, thinly sliced	2
2 cups	sliced button mushrooms	500 mL
1 tbsp	paprika	15 mL
1 tbsp	Dijon mustard	15 mL
1	14-oz/398 mL can tomatoes, with juices, chopped	1
1	sweet red pepper, seeded and thinly sliced	1
1	sweet green pepper, seeded and thinly sliced	1
½ tsp	salt	2 mL
¼ tsp	pepper	1 mL
1 cup	sour cream	250 mL

1. Cut each steak crosswise into four pieces.

2. In a large skillet, heat 1 tbsp/15 mL oil on high heat. Pat steaks dry and brown quickly, about 1 minute on each side. Remove steaks from skillet.

3. Add remaining 1 tbsp/15 mL oil to pan and reduce heat to medium-high. Add onions and mushrooms and cook for 5 minutes until softened. Stir in paprika, mustard, tomatoes, sweet peppers, steaks, salt and pepper. Cover and simmer for 15 minutes.

4. Gradually stir in sour cream. Heat through but do not boil. Adjust seasonings to taste. Serve over noodles.

Makes 5 to 6 servings
PREPARATION TIME: 12 minutes
COOKING TIME: 20 minutes

Roasted Beef Tenderloin with Mushroom Sauce

¼ cup	Dijon mustard	50 mL
2 tbsp	grated lemon rind	25 mL
1 tbsp	coarsely ground black peppercorns	15 mL
1 tbsp	olive oil	15 mL
1	2-lb/1 kg piece beef tenderloin	1

MUSHROOM SAUCE:

½ oz	dried porcini mushrooms (page 78)	15 g
1 cup	warm water	250 mL
2 tbsp	butter	25 mL
1	onion, diced	1
8 oz	button mushrooms, sliced	250 g
8 oz	portobello mushrooms, trimmed and sliced	250 g
1 cup	whipping cream	250 mL
	Salt and pepper to taste	
2 tbsp	chopped fresh parsley	25 mL

1. In a small bowl, combine mustard, lemon rind, peppercorns and oil. Rub marinade over beef. Let stand for 30 minutes.

2. Place beef on a rack in a shallow roasting pan. Roast in a preheated 425°F/220°C oven for 20 minutes. Reduce heat to 350°F/180°C and continue roasting for 30 minutes until a meat thermometer registers 140°F/60°C for medium-rare. Let roast rest for 10 minutes before carving.

3. Meanwhile, to prepare mushroom sauce, place dried porcini mushrooms in a small bowl and cover with warm water. Let soften for 20 minutes. Strain soaking liquid through clean dishcloth or coffee filter and reserve. Rinse mushrooms if they are sandy. Chop and reserve.

4. Melt butter in a skillet over medium-high heat. Add onion, button and portobello mushrooms and reserved porcini mushrooms. Cook for 8 minutes until softened. Add reserved mushroom liquid and cream. Increase heat to high and cook for 6 minutes until sauce is slightly thickened. Season to taste with salt and pepper. Stir in parsley. Keep warm. Carve tenderloin and serve with mushroom sauce.

Makes 6 to 8 servings
PREPARATION TIME: 30 minutes to marinate beef and prepare mushrooms; 12 minutes to prepare sauce
COOKING TIME: 50 minutes plus standing time

Fresh Mushrooms

Fresh mushrooms should be plump and firm. Remove them from their plastic wrapping as soon as possible and store them in a paper bag or loosely wrapped in the refrigerator. To prepare, wipe them clean with a damp towel or, if they are very dirty, rinse them very quickly under running water. The tough stems of mushrooms like shiitakes should be removed (discard them, or use them in stocks).

Cook mushrooms at fairly high heat just until they soften and start to lose their juices. Do not overcook them (in stir-fries, add them to the wok or skillet toward the end of the cooking time). Large portobello mushrooms can be steamed or barbecued whole like burgers.

Beef and Vegetable Stir-fry

½ cup	storebought or homemade stir-fry sauce	125 mL
⅔ cup	orange juice	150 mL
1 tsp	cornstarch	5 mL
2 tbsp	vegetable oil, divided	25 mL
12 oz	boneless top sirloin stir-fry strips	375 g
1	onion, thinly sliced	1
2	carrots, peeled and thinly sliced	2
2	stalks celery, thinly sliced	2
2 cups	broccoli florets	500 mL
1	sweet red pepper, seeded and thinly sliced	1
1 cup	snow peas, trimmed	250 mL

1. In a small bowl, combine stir-fry sauce, orange juice and cornstarch.

2. Heat 1 tbsp/15 mL oil in a wok or non-stick skillet over high heat. Add beef strips and stir-fry for 2 minutes until pinkness disappears. Remove and reserve.

3. Heat remaining 1 tbsp/15 mL oil in pan. Add onion, carrots and celery. Stir-fry for 3 minutes. Add broccoli and sweet pepper. Cover and cook for 2 minutes. Stir in snow peas and beef. Cook for 2 minutes.

4. Add sauce mixture to beef and vegetables. Cook for 2 minutes, stirring to coat with sauce. Serve with rice.

Makes 5 to 6 servings
PREPARATION TIME: 10 minutes
COOKING TIME: 12 minutes

Stir-frying Tips

- *Have all ingredients, and the stir-fry sauce, ready before you start cooking. Stir-fried dishes should be cooked quickly so the ingredients retain their colour and crispness.*

- *Cut all ingredients into even, same-sized pieces.*

- *Heat the oil on medium-high to high heat but reduce the temperature if there is any sign of smoking.*

- *Use a vegetable oil with a high smoking point, such as corn, safflower or peanut oil. If food sticks while you are cooking, add a little water to the pan.*

- *Stir-fry seasoning sauces can be made from scratch or bought already prepared. Stir up the sauce just before adding it to the pan.*

- *Serve stir-fried dishes as soon as they are cooked.*

Veal Scallopini Piccata

2 tbsp	olive oil (or more)	25 mL
1½ lb	veal scallopini, pounded thin (page 35)	750 g
¾ cup	dry white wine or chicken stock	175 mL
2 tbsp	balsamic vinegar	25 mL
¼ cup	whipping cream (optional)	50 mL
¼ tsp	salt	1 mL
¼ tsp	pepper	1 mL
¼ cup	chopped fresh parsley	50 mL
	Lemon slices	

1. Heat oil in a large non-stick skillet over high heat. Pat veal dry and cook in batches, about 1 to 2 minutes per side, until golden. Transfer to a serving platter.

2. Add wine, vinegar and cream to skillet. Cook for 2 minutes until slightly thickened. Add salt and pepper.

3. Pour sauce over veal. Serve garnished with parsley and lemon slices.

Makes 4 to 6 servings
PREPARATION TIME: 6 minutes
COOKING TIME: 10 to 15 minutes

Veal Chops with Cranberry Relish

CRANBERRY RELISH:

1 cup	cranberries, fresh or frozen and defrosted, coarsely chopped	250 mL
4	green onions, finely chopped	4
2 tbsp	liquid honey	25 mL
2 tbsp	cider vinegar	25 mL
2 tbsp	orange juice concentrate	25 mL
2 tsp	chopped fresh sage (or ½ tsp/2 mL dried)	10 mL
¼ cup	olive oil	50 mL
16	whole fresh sage leaves (optional)	16
4	veal loin chops, ¾ inch/2 cm thick	4
¼ tsp	salt	1 mL
¼ tsp	pepper	1 mL
½ cup	chopped shallots	125 mL
½ cup	chicken stock or white wine	125 mL

Shallots

Shallots look like small elongated onions, but they are milder and sweeter than most onions. They add a slight garlic flavour to sauces and stuffings. If you can't find them, substitute regular onions and a bit of chopped garlic.

1. To prepare relish, in a mixing bowl, combine cranberries, green onions, honey, vinegar, orange juice concentrate and chopped sage.

2. Heat oil in a non-stick skillet on medium-high heat. Add sage leaves and fry for 30 seconds. Remove to paper towels to drain.

3. Pour off all but 1 tbsp/15 mL oil. Pat veal chops dry and season with salt and pepper. Cook for 4 to 5 minutes per side. Remove to a serving platter.

4. Add shallots to pan. Cook for 30 seconds until softened. Add stock and cook for 1 minute.

5. Pour sauce over chops. Serve with fried sage leaves and relish.

Makes 4 servings
PREPARATION TIME: 12 minutes
COOKING TIME: 12 minutes

Veal with Tomato Zucchini Sauce

TOMATO ZUCCHINI SAUCE:

2 tbsp	olive oil	25 mL
2	onions, chopped	2
2	cloves garlic, finely chopped	2
1	28-oz/796 mL can plum tomatoes, pureed with juices	1
3	medium zucchini, diced	3
1 tbsp	chopped fresh sage (or 1 tsp/5 mL dried)	15 mL
½ tsp	salt	2 mL
¼ tsp	pepper	1 mL

½ cup	all-purpose flour	125 mL
½ tsp	salt	2 mL
¼ tsp	pepper	1 mL
1½ lb	veal scallopini, pounded thin (page 35)	750 g
2 tbsp	butter	25 mL
2 tbsp	olive oil	25 mL

1. Heat olive oil in a saucepan on medium-high heat. Add onions and cook for 3 minutes until starting to colour. Add garlic and cook for 1 minute.

2. Stir in tomatoes, zucchini, sage, salt and pepper. Bring to a boil. Reduce heat and simmer for 20 minutes until thickened. Adjust seasonings to taste. Keep sauce warm.

3. Combine flour, salt and pepper in a shallow dish. Dip veal in seasoned flour, shaking off excess.

4. Heat butter and oil in a large skillet over medium-high heat. Cook veal in batches until golden, about 1 to 2 minutes per side.

5. Arrange veal on a serving platter. Pour hot sauce over veal.

Makes 6 servings
PREPARATION TIME: 15 minutes
COOKING TIME: 30 minutes

Herbed Leg of Lamb with Roasted Sweet Potatoes

½ cup	chopped shallots	125 mL
½ cup	chopped fresh parsley	125 mL
½ cup	fresh or dry breadcrumbs	125 mL
¼ cup	balsamic vinegar	50 mL
2 tbsp	liquid honey	25 mL
2 tbsp	olive oil	25 mL
2 tbsp	Dijon mustard	25 mL
1 tbsp	chopped fresh rosemary (or ½ tsp/2 mL dried)	15 mL
¼ tsp	salt	1 mL
¼ tsp	pepper	1 mL
1	4-lb/2 kg butterflied boneless leg of lamb, trimmed	1
4	large sweet potatoes (2½ lb/1.2 kg), peeled and cut in 2-inch/5 cm pieces	4

1. In a small bowl, combine shallots, parsley, breadcrumbs, vinegar, honey, oil, mustard, rosemary, salt and pepper.

2. Pour three-quarters of marinade over lamb. Rub mixture in. Marinate lamb, refrigerated, for 2 hours.

3. Place potatoes in large bowl. Add remaining marinade and mix to coat potatoes.

4. Place lamb cut side down on a lightly oiled roasting pan or baking sheet. Place potatoes in lightly oiled foil-lined baking pan. Roast lamb and potatoes in a preheated 375°F/190°C oven for 30 to 35 minutes or until a meat thermometer in lamb registers 140°F/60°C for medium-well. Remove lamb from oven and let rest in a warm place for 10 minutes while potatoes finish roasting. Carve lamb and serve with sweet potatoes.

Makes 6 to 8 servings
PREPARATION TIME: 10 minutes plus 2 hours marinating time
COOKING TIME: 45 minutes

Lamb

Fresh domestic lamb is most plentiful between late spring and fall, but imported lamb from New Zealand and Australia is available year round. Spring lamb is the most tender and comes from animals younger than five months. Boneless legs are ideal for roasting or barbecuing; the T-bone-shaped loin chops are the meatiest chops. Broil or grill them about 3 inches from the heat.

To prepare lamb, trim the fat and take off as much of the white papery skin (fell) as you can remove easily.

Grilled Lamb Chops with Jalapeño Mint Sauce

JALAPEÑO MINT SAUCE:

½ cup	apple juice	125 mL
¼ cup	cider vinegar or white wine vinegar	50 mL
2 tbsp	liquid honey	25 mL
1 cup	chopped fresh mint	250 mL
½	jalapeño pepper, seeded and finely chopped	½
¼ tsp	salt	1 mL
¼ tsp	pepper	1 mL
1 tbsp	olive oil	15 mL
2	cloves garlic, minced	2
2 tsp	chopped fresh oregano or savory (or ½ tsp/2 mL dried)	10 mL
¼ tsp	pepper	1 mL
8	loin lamb chops, 1 inch/2.5 cm thick, trimmed	8
	Salt	

1. Pour apple juice, vinegar and honey into a small saucepan. Bring to a boil, reduce heat and simmer for 15 minutes. Turn off heat and stir in mint leaves, jalapeño, salt and pepper. Refrigerate if not serving within 3 hours.

2. In a small bowl, combine oil, garlic, oregano and pepper. Pour over chops and rub into surface.

3. To cook chops, preheat grill, non-stick pan or broiler. Sprinkle chops with salt. Cook over high heat for 5 to 6 minutes per side for medium-rare. Serve with mint sauce.

Makes 4 to 6 servings
PREPARATION TIME: 20 minutes
COOKING TIME: 12 minutes

Sautéed Pork Chops with Apples

3 tbsp	olive oil, divided	45 mL
8	fast-fry centre-cut pork chops, trimmed	8
¼ tsp	salt	1 mL
¼ tsp	pepper	1 mL
1	onion, sliced	1
2	cloves garlic, finely chopped	2
3	large apples, thickly sliced	3
2 tsp	chopped fresh thyme (or ¼ tsp/1 mL dried)	10 mL
½ cup	apple juice	125 mL
½ cup	whipping cream	125 mL
2 tbsp	chopped fresh parsley	25 mL

1. Heat 2 tbsp/25 mL oil in a large skillet over high heat. Pat pork chops dry and cook for 4 minutes per side until brown. Remove from pan to serving dish and sprinkle with salt and pepper. Keep warm.

2. Reduce heat under skillet to medium and heat remaining 1 tbsp/15 mL oil. Add onion, garlic and apple slices. Cook for 4 minutes until apples are just tender. Stir gently to avoid breaking apples.

3. Add thyme, apple juice and whipping cream to skillet (for a lower-fat version, omit whipping cream and increase apple juice to 1 cup/250 mL). Cook for 4 minutes until sauce is slightly thickened.

4. To serve, spoon apples and sauce over pork chops and sprinkle with parsley.

Makes 4 to 6 servings
PREPARATION TIME: 10 minutes
COOKING TIME: 15 minutes

Stuffed Pork Tenderloin with Barbecue Glaze

2 tbsp	olive oil, divided	25 mL
½ cup	diced onion	125 mL
½ cup	diced celery	125 mL
1	carrot, peeled and diced	1
3	slices stale bread, cut in cubes (about 1½ cups/375 mL)	3
¼ cup	orange juice or apple juice	50 mL
¼ tsp	dried sage	1 mL
¼ tsp	salt	1 mL
¼ tsp	pepper	1 mL
2	pork tenderloins (12 oz/375 g each)	2
½ cup	storebought or homemade barbecue sauce	125 mL

1. In a small skillet, heat 1 tbsp/15 mL oil over medium heat. Add onion, celery and carrot. Cook for 4 minutes until softened. Place in a mixing bowl.

2. Add bread cubes, juice, sage, salt and pepper to bowl and combine well.

3. Cut each pork tenderloin lengthwise most of the way through so it can open and lie flat. Flatten to ¼-inch/5 mm thickness with a meat pounder or mallet.

4. Lay one tenderloin, cut side up, on flat surface. Arrange stuffing over surface, mounding in centre.

5. Place remaining tenderloin over stuffing with small end to large end of bottom tenderloin to create a more even "roast." Tie tenderloins at intervals with kitchen twine or skewer edges together.

6. In a non-stick skillet, heat remaining 1 tbsp/15 mL oil over medium-high heat. Add meat and brown entire surface, about 6 to 8 minutes. Place on foil- or parchment-lined baking sheet. Spoon barbecue sauce over meat.

7. Bake tenderloin in preheated 350°F/180°C oven for 35 minutes. Turn and baste several times during baking. Let stand for 5 minutes before slicing.

Makes 6 servings
PREPARATION TIME: 15 minutes
COOKING TIME: 45 minutes

Maple-glazed Ham Steaks with Pineapple

4	**Black Forest ham steaks (6 oz/175 g each)**	4
4	**slices fresh pineapple**	4
½ cup	**maple syrup**	125 mL
1 tbsp	**Dijon mustard**	15 mL
1 tbsp	**white vinegar or cider vinegar**	15 mL
¼ tsp	**ground cinnamon**	1 mL

1. Arrange ham and pineapple slices on a foil-lined baking sheet.

2. In a small bowl, combine maple syrup, mustard, vinegar and cinnamon. Spoon glaze over ham and pineapple.

3. Place ham and pineapple under a preheated broiler and cook for 4 minutes per side until bubbling and starting to brown.

Makes 4 servings
PREPARATION TIME: 5 minutes
COOKING TIME: 8 minutes

Pineapple

Look for Golden Pineapple, a relatively new variety with bright-yellow flesh. It is often sweeter and juicier than other varieties. Peel the pineapple with a large, sharp knife, cut the fruit crosswise into slices and remove the core using the tip of the knife. Use any leftover pineapple in fruit salads.

Menus

Easy Family Dinner

Sautéed Pork Chops with Apples (page 55)

Savoy Cabbage Slaw with Prosciutto Dressing (page 22)

Creamy Mashed Potatoes (page 109)

Fresh Fruit

Teen Vegetarian Buffet

(no utensils required!)

Spinach and Feta Phyllo Spirals (page 15)

Potato and Zucchini Pizza with Arugula Pesto (page 64)

Greek Salad Pitas (page 92)

Triple Chocolate Chip Cookies (page 120)

Meatless Main Courses

Harvest Vegetable and Lentil Soup

Ratatouille and Chickpea Casserole

Braised Lentils

Broccoli and Tofu with Thai Peanut Sauce

Potato and Zucchini Pizza with Arugula Pesto

Orzo Salad with Feta

Gnocchi with Broccoli and Gorgonzola Sauce

Eggplant and Bocconcini Sandwiches

Savoury Onion Bread Pudding
with Tomato Relish

Red Pepper, Zucchini and Cheddar Quiche

Harvest Vegetable and Lentil Soup

2 tbsp	olive oil	25 mL
2	onions, chopped	2
2	stalks celery, diced	2
2	parsnips, peeled and diced	2
2	carrots, peeled and diced	2
1	sweet potato, peeled and diced	1
1 cup	dry red lentils	250 mL
2 tbsp	tomato paste	25 mL
8 cups	vegetable stock	2 L
1 tsp	chopped fresh thyme (or ¼ tsp/1 mL dried)	5 mL
1	bay leaf	1
¾ tsp	salt	4 mL
½ tsp	pepper	2 mL
½ cup	small-sized pasta (e.g., small shells)	125 mL
¼ cup	chopped fresh parsley	50 mL
⅓ cup	grated Asiago cheese	75 mL

Lentils

Like all legumes, lentils are an excellent source of protein as well as being economical and low in fat. Unlike many other dried legumes, however, lentils do not need to be presoaked. Split red or orange lentils lose their shape when cooked and are good in soups and purees; whole green or brown lentils are slightly larger and retain their shape and texture when cooked — use them in salads.

To prepare dry lentils, rinse them in cold water and pick out any discoloured or shrivelled bits before cooking.

1. Heat oil in a large saucepan on medium-high heat. Add onions and cook for 5 minutes until lightly browned. Add celery, parsnips and carrots. Cook for 5 minutes.

2. Add potato, lentils, tomato paste, stock, thyme and bay leaf. Bring to a boil. Reduce heat. Cover and simmer for 30 minutes until lentils and vegetables are just tender. Add salt and pepper.

3. Add pasta and cook for 8 minutes until just tender. Taste and adjust seasonings.

4. Add parsley and serve with cheese.

Makes 8 to 10 servings
PREPARATION TIME: 15 minutes
COOKING TIME: 50 minutes

Ratatouille and Chickpea Casserole

4 tbsp	olive oil, divided	50 mL
2	onions, thinly sliced	2
2	cloves garlic, finely chopped	2
¼ tsp	hot red pepper flakes	1 mL
1	medium eggplant, diced	1
2	sweet red peppers, seeded and diced	2
2	medium zucchini, diced	2
4	tomatoes, diced	4
½ tsp	dried thyme	2 mL
½ tsp	salt	2 mL
¼ tsp	pepper	1 mL
1	19-oz/540 mL can chickpeas, rinsed and drained	1
½ cup	fresh breadcrumbs	125 mL
¾ cup	crumbled goat cheese (chèvre)	175 mL

1. In a large saucepan, heat 2 tbsp/25 mL oil over medium-high heat. Add onions. Cook for 6 to 7 minutes or until golden. Add garlic and hot pepper flakes. Cook for 1 minute.

2. Add eggplant, red peppers and zucchini to saucepan. Cook for 6 minutes, stirring frequently. Add tomatoes, thyme, salt and pepper. Cover and cook over medium heat for 20 minutes, stirring occasionally.

3. Add chickpeas to saucepan and combine. Taste and adjust seasonings. Place ratatouille in a lightly oiled 13 x 9-inch/3.5 L baking dish.

4. In a small bowl, combine breadcrumbs, goat cheese and remaining 2 tbsp/25 mL oil. Sprinkle over surface. Bake in a preheated 375°F/190°C oven for 25 minutes until bubbling and top is golden.

Makes 6 servings
PREPARATION TIME: 12 minutes
COOKING TIME: 60 minutes

Braised Lentils

2 tbsp	olive oil	25 mL
2	leeks, trimmed and diced	2
2	cloves garlic, finely chopped	2
2	stalks celery, diced	2
3	carrots, peeled and diced	3
1	19-oz/540 mL can lentils, drained and rinsed	1
1 cup	vegetable stock	250 mL
2 tbsp	tomato paste	25 mL
2 tbsp	chopped sun-dried tomatoes (page 20)	25 mL
1 tsp	chopped fresh thyme (or ½ tsp/2 mL dried)	5 mL
½ tsp	salt	2 mL
¼ tsp	pepper	1 mL
¼ cup	chopped fresh cilantro (page 39)	50 mL
½ cup	grated Monterey Jack cheese	125 mL

Leeks

To prepare leeks, remove any tough outer layers and cut off the dark-green leaves at the top. Trim the root end and split the leek lengthwise. Carefully rinse out any dirt trapped between the layers. If the leeks are very sandy, chop them, place in a bowl of water for a few minutes, and then lift them out with a strainer once the sand has settled to the bottom of the bowl.

1. In a large saucepan, heat oil over medium-high heat. Add leeks and garlic. Cook for 3 minutes until softened. Add celery and carrots. Cook for 5 minutes.

2. Stir in lentils, stock, tomato paste, sun-dried tomatoes, thyme, salt and pepper. Bring to a boil. Reduce heat and simmer, covered, for 10 minutes. Remove cover and continue cooking for 5 to 8 minutes or until most of moisture evaporates.

3. To serve, sprinkle with cilantro and cheese. Serve with cooked rice or crusty bread.

Makes 4 to 5 servings
PREPARATION TIME: 15 minutes
COOKING TIME: 30 minutes

Broccoli and Tofu with Thai Peanut Sauce

THAI PEANUT SAUCE:

1 tbsp	finely chopped fresh ginger (page 46)	15 mL
2	green onions, chopped	2
¼ cup	packed fresh cilantro leaves (page 39)	50 mL
¼ cup	peanut butter	50 mL
2 tbsp	soy sauce	25 mL
2 tbsp	lime juice	25 mL
2 tsp	granulated sugar	10 mL
1 tsp	sesame oil (page 13)	5 mL
¼ cup	water	50 mL
2 tbsp	vegetable oil, divided	25 mL
2 tbsp	finely chopped fresh ginger	25 mL
3	cloves garlic, finely chopped	3
4	green onions, chopped	4
1	bunch broccoli, cut into florets, stems trimmed and sliced diagonally	1
12 oz	extra-firm tofu, cut in ½-inch/1 cm cubes	375 g

Tofu

Tofu is soybean curd and is usually sold in water-packed blocks. To keep it fresh, change the packing water daily.

There are many different kinds of tofu, ranging from soft to extra-firm. Firm or extra-firm is best for grilled dishes and stir-fries. Rinse the tofu under cold water and pat dry before using.

1. In a food processor or blender, combine ginger, green onions, cilantro, peanut butter, soy sauce, lime juice, sugar, sesame oil and water. Blend until smooth. Pour into a small saucepan and warm over low heat. Keep warm.

2. Heat 1 tbsp/15 mL oil in a large skillet or wok on high heat. Add ginger, garlic and green onions. Stir-fry for 30 seconds.

3. Add broccoli to skillet and stir-fry for 5 minutes until tender-crisp. Remove vegetables and reserve.

4. Add remaining 1 tbsp/15 mL oil to skillet. Add tofu and stir-fry for 3 minutes until heated through.

5. Return vegetables to skillet and toss lightly to combine. Spoon tofu and broccoli onto serving platter. Pour warm peanut sauce over and toss gently. Serve with steamed rice.

Makes 4 to 6 servings
PREPARATION TIME: 15 minutes
COOKING TIME: 15 minutes

Potato and Zucchini Pizza with Arugula Pesto

1	26-oz/750 g package prepared pizza dough	1
4 tbsp	olive oil, divided	50 mL
1 tbsp	cornmeal	15 mL
8 oz	potatoes (2 medium), scrubbed and very thinly sliced	250 g
2	medium zucchini, very thinly sliced	2
½ tsp	salt	2 mL
¼ tsp	pepper	1 mL
¾ cup	storebought or homemade arugula pesto or basil pesto	175 mL

1. On a lightly floured surface, roll pizza dough into a 14-inch/35 cm circle.

2. Brush a pizza pan or baking sheet with 2 tbsp/25 mL olive oil. Dust with cornmeal. Place pizza dough on pan, reshaping if necessary. If dough is springy, let rest for a few minutes before reshaping.

3. In a mixing bowl, toss potato and zucchini slices with salt, pepper and ¼ cup/50 mL pesto. Arrange over dough. Let stand at room temperature for 15 minutes.

4. Bake pizza in a preheated 400°F/200°C oven for 30 to 35 minutes or until potatoes are almost tender.

5. Spread remaining ½ cup/125 mL pesto over surface and drizzle with remaining 2 tbsp/25 mL oil. Continue baking for 5 to 8 minutes or until golden. Remove from pan onto a cooling rack. Serve warm or at room temperature.

Makes 8 to 12 pieces
PREPARATION TIME: 10 minutes plus 15 minutes rising time
COOKING TIME: 45 minutes

Photo (opposite): Steak Teriyaki (see recipe page 46) and Springtime Asparagus (see recipe page 100)

Photo (overleaf): Sautéed Pork Chops with Apples (see recipe page 55) and Creamy Mashed Potatoes (see recipe page 109)

Orzo Salad with Feta

1½ cups	orzo pasta	375 mL
1	English cucumber, quartered, seeded and thinly sliced	1
½	sweet onion (e.g., Vidalia or Spanish) thinly sliced	½
4	plum tomatoes, seeded and diced	4
¼ cup	chopped fresh dill	50 mL
¼ cup	chopped fresh mint	50 mL
2 tbsp	chopped fresh oregano (or ½ tsp/2 mL dried)	25 mL
¼ cup	olive oil	50 mL
¼ cup	lemon juice	50 mL
1 tsp	salt	5 mL
¼ tsp	pepper	1 mL
1¼ cups	crumbled feta cheese (6 oz/175 g)	300 mL

Orzo

Orzo is a small rice-shaped pasta. It can be served in place of rice, as a side dish, or it can be used in soups and salads.

1. Cook orzo in a large amount of boiling salted water for 6 minutes or just until tender. Drain and rinse under cold water. Drain well.

2. In a large mixing bowl, combine orzo, cucumber, onion, tomatoes, dill, mint, oregano, oil, lemon juice, salt and pepper. Toss well.

3. Add feta to salad. Let stand at room temperature for 30 minutes or refrigerate for up to 6 hours (remove from refrigerator 1 hour before serving). Toss again before serving and adjust seasonings if necessary.

Makes 6 servings
PREPARATION TIME: 15 minutes
COOKING TIME: 8 minutes

Photo (overleaf): Spaghetti with Rapini, Potatoes and Tomato Sauce (see recipe page 77)

Photo (opposite): Cornmeal Blueberry Pancakes with Maple Yogurt Sauce (see recipe page 85)

Gnocchi with Broccoli and Gorgonzola Sauce

Broccoli

Look for bunches with compact, dark-green florets and firm stalks without woody stems or yellowing branches. To prepare broccoli, remove any large leaves. Trim off the tough bases and peel partway up the stems if they are thick. Then slice the stems and separate the heads into florets.

Store broccoli in the refrigerator for up to three days.

½ cup	whipping cream	125 mL
¼ cup	milk	50 mL
2 tbsp	butter	25 mL
4 oz	Gorgonzola, blue cheese or Roquefort cheese	125 g
¼ tsp	salt	1 mL
¼ tsp	pepper	1 mL
8 oz	gnocchi or shell-shaped pasta (3 cups/750 mL)	250 g
1	bunch broccoli, trimmed and cut in florets	1
¼ cup	chopped fresh chives	50 mL

1. In a large saucepan, heat cream, milk and butter on medium heat. Crumble in Gorgonzola. Add salt and pepper. Keep sauce warm over low heat.

2. Meanwhile, cook pasta in boiling water until almost tender, about 8 minutes. Add broccoli for the last 3 minutes. Drain pasta and broccoli well.

3. Add pasta and broccoli to warm sauce. Toss well. Taste and adjust seasoning. Serve garnished with chives.

Makes 4 to 6 servings
PREPARATION TIME: 5 minutes
COOKING TIME: 15 minutes

Eggplant and Bocconcini Sandwiches

1	large eggplant (1¼ lb/625 g), cut in ¼-inch/5 mm slices	1
3 tbsp	olive oil, divided	45 mL
8 oz	bocconcini cheese, cut in ¼-inch/5 mm slices	250 g
1	sweet red pepper, roasted (page 108), seeded and cut in strips	1
¼ cup	coarsely chopped black olives	50 mL
20	fresh basil leaves	20
1	small bunch arugula (page 19), broken in pieces	1
1 tbsp	red wine vinegar	15 mL
¼ tsp	salt	1 mL
¼ tsp	pepper	1 mL

1. Place eggplant slices on parchment-lined baking sheets and brush with 2 tbsp/25 mL oil. Bake in a preheated 400°F/200°C oven for 12 to 15 minutes or until golden and tender, turning once and brushing with oil.

2. Arrange bocconcini slices, pepper strips, olives and basil on half the eggplant slices. Top with remaining eggplant.

3. Return to oven and bake for 8 minutes until cheese starts to melt. Remove and let stand for 10 to 15 minutes before serving.

4. Meanwhile, in large bowl, toss arugula with vinegar, remaining 1 tbsp/15 mL oil, salt and pepper.

5. Arrange arugula on serving dishes. Place whole or halved sandwiches over arugula.

Makes 6 servings
PREPARATION TIME: 12 minutes
COOKING TIME: 25 minutes plus standing time

Savoury Onion Bread Pudding with Tomato Relish

2 tbsp	olive oil	25 mL
3	onions, chopped	3
2	cloves garlic, finely chopped	2
2	stalks celery, diced	2
8 oz	button mushrooms, sliced (3 cups/750 mL)	250 g
¼ cup	chopped fresh parsley	50 mL
2 tbsp	chopped fresh sage (or ½ tsp/2 mL dried)	25 mL
6	slices stale bread, cut in cubes (5 cups/1.25 L)	6
1 cup	grated old Cheddar cheese	250 mL
1½ cups	vegetable stock	375 mL
½ cup	milk	125 mL
3	eggs, beaten	3
½ tsp	salt	2 mL
¼ tsp	pepper	1 mL
¼ cup	grated Parmesan cheese	50 mL

TOMATO RELISH:

3	tomatoes, seeded and chopped	3
1	sweet red pepper, seeded and diced	1
1	sweet yellow pepper, seeded and diced	1
2	green onions, chopped	2
2 tsp	chopped fresh herbs (e.g., basil, marjoram and/or oregano)	10 mL
2 tbsp	balsamic vinegar	25 mL
¼ tsp	salt	1 mL

1. Heat oil in a large skillet over medium-high heat. Add onions, garlic and celery. Cook for about 6 minutes until very soft and light golden.

2. Add mushrooms and cook for 4 minutes. Remove from heat. Add parsley and sage.

3. In a large mixing bowl, combine onion mixture, bread cubes, Cheddar, stock, milk, eggs, salt and pepper. Mix together completely.

4. Pour pudding mixture into an oiled 9-inch/2 L square baking dish. Sprinkle with Parmesan.

5. Bake in a preheated 350°F/180°C oven for 35 to 40 minutes or until golden-brown and puffed. Let stand for 10 minutes before serving.

6. Meanwhile, to prepare tomato relish, in a mixing bowl, combine tomatoes, sweet peppers, green onions, fresh herbs, vinegar and salt.

7. Cut pudding into squares and serve with relish.

Makes 6 to 8 servings
PREPARATION TIME: 25 minutes
COOKING TIME: 45 minutes plus standing time

Red Pepper, Zucchini and Cheddar Quiche

2 tbsp	butter	25 mL
½	onion, diced	½
1	medium zucchini, grated	1
1	sweet red pepper, seeded and diced	1
1 cup	grated old Cheddar cheese	250 mL
1	9-inch/23 cm deep pie shell, defrosted	1
2	eggs	2
¾ cup	sour cream or milk	175 mL
¼ tsp	salt	1 mL
2 tbsp	chopped fresh dill	25 mL

Zucchini

Zucchini are summer squash. The yellow and green varieties taste very similar, and can be used interchangeably. The smallest zucchini are the most tender and are best for using in salads or with dips.

Zucchini can be sliced like cucumbers or cut into French-fry shapes for sautés or stir-fries. Do not peel them unless the skin is tough. Large zucchini can be seeded, stuffed and baked.

1. Melt butter in a large skillet over medium heat. Add onion, zucchini and red pepper. Cook, stirring, for 8 minutes until tender. Remove from heat and cool slightly.

2. Spread vegetables and cheese in pie shell.

3. In a bowl, combine eggs, sour cream and salt. Pour over filling. Sprinkle with dill.

4. Bake in a preheated 425°F/220°C oven for 10 minutes. Reduce heat to 350°F/180°C and bake for 30 minutes longer until centre is set. Let stand for 10 minutes before serving.

Makes 6 servings
PREPARATION TIME: 8 minutes
COOKING TIME: 50 minutes plus standing time

Pasta, Rice and Polenta

Rotelle and Tomato Beef Bake

Orecchiette with Roasted Onions
and Butternut Squash

Thai-flavoured Noodles

Tortellini with Prosciutto and Peas

Penne with Tomatoes, Roasted Garlic and Basil

Spaghetti with Rapini, Potatoes
and Tomato Sauce

Farfalle and Mushroom Gratin

Chicken Fried Rice

Paella

Rice and Bulgur Pilaf

Polenta with Corn and Italian Sausage

Rotelle and Tomato Beef Bake

2 tbsp	olive oil	25 mL
2	stalks celery, diced	2
1	onion, chopped	1
4 oz	button mushrooms, sliced (1½ cups/375 mL)	125 g
¼ tsp	hot red pepper flakes	1 mL
1 lb	lean ground beef	500 g
2 cups	tomato sauce	500 mL
½ tsp	dried oregano	2 mL
½ tsp	dried rosemary	2 mL
1 tsp	salt	5 mL
¼ tsp	pepper	1 mL
8 oz	rotelle (wagon-wheel) or rotini pasta (3 cups/750 mL	250 g
8 oz	mozzarella cheese, diced	250 g
¼ cup	grated Romano cheese	125 mL

1. Heat oil in a large skillet over medium-high heat. Add celery, onion, mushrooms and hot pepper flakes. Cook for 2 minutes until softened

2. Increase heat to high. Add ground beef and cook for 4 minutes, stirring, until starting to brown.

3. Stir in tomato sauce, oregano, rosemary, salt and pepper. Reduce heat to medium and cook gently for 10 minutes.

4. Meanwhile, cook pasta in boiling water until tender but firm, about 8 minutes. Drain.

5. Combine sauce, pasta and mozzarella. Spoon into a lightly oiled 13 x 9-inch/3.5 L baking dish. Sprinkle with Romano. Bake in a preheated 375°F/190°C oven for 20 to 25 minutes or until bubbly.

Makes 8 servings
PREPARATION TIME: 10 minutes
COOKING TIME: 55 minutes

Orecchiette with Roasted Onions and Butternut Squash

1	large sweet onion (e.g. Vidalia or Spanish), peeled	1
1	small butternut squash, peeled and seeded	1
3 tbsp	olive oil	45 mL
2 tbsp	coarsely chopped fresh sage or thyme (or 1 tsp/5 mL dried)	25 mL
1 tsp	salt	5 mL
½ tsp	pepper	2 mL
8 oz	orecchiette pasta (3 cups/750 mL)	250 g
⅓ cup	grated Parmesan cheese	75 mL

1. Cut onion and squash into ½-inch/1 cm pieces to give a total yield of 7 cups/1.75 L.

2. In a large bowl, toss onion and squash with oil, sage, salt and pepper. Spread on a parchment-lined baking sheet and roast in a preheated 450°F/230°C oven for 35 minutes until vegetables are tender and golden. Stir occasionally during cooking time.

3. Meanwhile, cook pasta in boiling water until tender but firm. Reserve ½ cup/125 mL pasta liquid. Drain pasta.

4. Toss pasta with roasted vegetables and cheese, adding some pasta liquid if pasta seems too dry.

Makes 6 servings
PREPARATION TIME: 10 minutes
COOKING TIME: 35 minutes

Pasta-cooking Tips

- *Use a large pot and lots of water — 4 to 6 qt/L water for every pound of pasta.*

- *Add the pasta to rapidly boiling water and stir to separate.*

- *Once the pasta has come to a boil, cook uncovered, stirring occasionally to prevent the noodles from sticking.*

- *Always taste for doneness. For dried pasta, start testing about 5 minutes after the water returns to a boil. The pasta should be tender but still have some bite.*

- *Do not rinse pasta unless you are using it in a salad.*

Thai-flavoured Noodles

1	14-oz/400 mL can coconut milk	1
¼ cup	lime juice or lemon juice	50 mL
2 tbsp	soy sauce	25 mL
2 tbsp	oyster sauce	25 mL
2 tbsp	brown sugar	25 mL
1 tsp	hot red pepper sauce, or to taste	5 mL
2 tbsp	vegetable oil	25 mL
1	onion, thinly sliced	1
2	cloves garlic, finely chopped	2
8 oz	green beans, sliced diagonally	250 g
1	sweet red pepper, seeded and thinly sliced	1
1	400-g package cooked wheat noodles, rinsed and prepared according to package directions	1
¼ cup	fresh cilantro leaves (page 39)	50 mL
2	green onions, sliced diagonally	2
2 tbsp	chopped peanuts (optional)	25 mL

Cooked Wheat Noodles

There are many different kinds of ready-to-use Asian noodles. Some are precooked and just need rinsing, some (e.g., chow mein noodles) need to be immersed in boiling water for a few minutes before using, and some need to be completely cooked. If you can't find one kind, substitute another and follow the package directions.

1. In a bowl, combine coconut milk, lime juice, soy sauce, oyster sauce, brown sugar and hot pepper sauce.

2. Heat oil in a wok over medium-high heat. Add onion and garlic. Stir-fry until softened and fragrant, about 2 minutes. Increase heat to high. Add beans and red pepper and stir-fry for 3 minutes until vegetables are tender-crisp.

3. Add noodles and reserved sauce. Toss mixture well and turn into a serving dish. Serve garnished with cilantro, green onions and peanuts.

Makes 6 servings
PREPARATION TIME: 10 minutes
COOKING TIME: 10 minutes

Tortellini with Prosciutto and Peas

2 tbsp	olive oil	25 mL
1	small red onion, thinly sliced	1
2	cloves garlic, finely chopped	2
6 oz	thick prosciutto slices, cut in ¼-inch/5 mm dice	175 g
1 lb	fresh or frozen cheese tortellini	500 g
2 cups	frozen peas, defrosted	500 mL
⅓ cup	grated Parmesan cheese	75 mL

1. Heat oil in a large skillet on medium-high heat. Add onion and garlic. Cook until softened, about 5 minutes. Add prosciutto and cook for 4 minutes.

2. Meanwhile, bring a large saucepan of water to a boil and cook tortellini according to package directions. Drain pasta, reserving ¼ cup/50 mL cooking water.

3. Toss tortellini with prosciutto, peas and pasta water and heat through. Serve sprinkled with grated Parmesan.

Makes 4 to 6 servings
PREPARATION TIME: 8 minutes
COOKING TIME: 15 minutes

Penne with Tomatoes, Roasted Garlic and Basil

3	heads garlic	3
	Olive oil	
6	tomatoes, seeded and coarsely chopped	6
½ cup	shredded fresh basil leaves	125 mL
½ cup	coarsely chopped black olives	125 mL
3 tbsp	olive oil	45 mL
½ tsp	salt	2 mL
¼ tsp	pepper	1 mL
12 oz	penne pasta (4 cups/1 L)	375 g

1. Cut top quarter off each head of garlic or enough to expose each clove. Brush cut edges with olive oil and place cut side down on a small foil-lined pie plate. Roast in a preheated 375°F/190°C oven for 35 to 40 minutes or until garlic is soft when squeezed. Cool to room temperature. (This can be done up to 3 days in advance. Keep the roasted garlic covered in the refrigerator.)

2. In a large shallow serving bowl, squeeze roasted garlic out of skins. Mash with a fork. Add tomatoes, basil, olives, oil, salt and pepper. Toss well to incorporate mashed garlic.

3. Meanwhile, cook pasta in boiling water until tender but firm. Drain well. Add to tomato mixture. Toss well and serve immediately or let cool for 1 hour.

Makes 6 servings
PREPARATION TIME: 10 minutes
COOKING TIME: 40 minutes to roast garlic, plus 10 minutes

Basil

If you are not using fresh basil right away, stick the stems in a glass of water, cover the leaves loosely with a plastic bag to help retain humidity and store in the refrigerator. If you are not planning to use the basil within a few days, chop or shred it and cover with olive oil. Or freeze-dry the basil by spreading the chopped leaves on a baking sheet in the freezer. When frozen, place the basil in a tightly sealed container and keep frozen to use in cooked dishes and sauces.

Wash basil and pat or spin dry gently before using, as the leaves bruise easily. To cut fresh basil, roll up the leaves and slice very thinly. You'll end up with delicate shreds, and the leaves will not discolour as easily as they will when chopped.

Spaghetti with Rapini, Potatoes and Tomato Sauce

TOMATO SAUCE:

1	28-oz/796 mL can plum tomatoes, pureed with juices	1
¼ tsp	hot red pepper flakes	1 mL
1 tsp	chopped fresh oregano (or ½ tsp/2 mL dried)	5 mL
1 tsp	chopped fresh rosemary (or ½ tsp/2 mL dried)	5 mL
½ tsp	salt	2 mL
¼ tsp	pepper	1 mL
12 oz	spaghetti	375 g
2	medium potatoes, peeled and diced	2
1	bunch rapini, trimmed and coarsely chopped	1
2 tbsp	olive oil	25 mL
½ cup	whipping cream or pasta cooking liquid	125 mL
½ cup	grated Romano or Parmesan cheese	125 mL

1. Place tomatoes, hot pepper flakes, oregano, rosemary, salt and pepper in a saucepan. Bring to a boil. Reduce heat to medium and cook for 15 minutes, stirring occasionally.

2. Meanwhile, cook spaghetti and potatoes together in boiling water until almost tender, about 8 minutes. Add rapini and cook for 5 minutes. Drain pasta and vegetables, reserving ½ cup/125 mL cooking liquid if using.

3. Stir oil and cream into sauce. Cook for 5 minutes.

4. Toss pasta and vegetables with tomato sauce and cheese.

Makes 6 servings
PREPARATION TIME: 10 minutes
COOKING TIME: 20 minutes

Farfalle and Mushroom Gratin

½ oz	dried porcini mushrooms	15 g
½ cup	warm water	125 mL
¼ cup	butter	50 mL
1	small onion, chopped	1
8 oz	button mushrooms, sliced	125 g
¼ cup	all-purpose flour	50 mL
2 cups	chicken stock, hot	500 mL
1 cup	milk, hot	250 mL
¼ cup	chopped fresh parsley	50 mL
½ tsp	salt	2 mL
¼ tsp	pepper	1 mL
12 oz	farfalle (bow-tie) pasta (5 cups/1.25 L)	375 g
¼ cup	grated Parmesan cheese	50 mL

Dried Mushrooms

To reconstitute dried mushrooms, place them in a small bowl and cover with warm water. Let sit for 20 minutes. Rinse off the mushrooms, reserving the soaking liquid, and chop or slice to use in the recipe. Strain the soaking liquid (which contains a great deal of the mushroom flavour) through a coffee filter, clean dishcloth or cheesecloth to remove any grit and use it as part of the liquid in the recipe.

1. In a small bowl, soak dried mushrooms in warm water for 20 minutes. Strain mushrooms through cheesecloth or coffee filter, reserving liquid. Rinse mushrooms and chop.

2. In a saucepan, melt butter on medium heat. Add onion and fresh mushrooms and cook until softened, about 5 minutes. Stir in flour and cook, stirring, for 4 minutes.

3. Remove saucepan from heat. Stir in reserved mushroom juice and porcini mushrooms, stock and milk. Return to medium-high heat. Bring sauce to a boil, stirring to prevent sticking. Reduce heat to medium and cook sauce until thickened, about 8 minutes. Remove from heat. Add parsley, salt and pepper.

4. Meanwhile, cook farfalle in boiling water until tender but firm. Drain and combine with sauce. (There may appear to be too much sauce, but pasta will absorb it during baking.) Pour into a shallow 8-cup/2 L baking dish. Sprinkle with Parmesan. Bake in a preheated 375°F/190°C for 30 minutes until bubbly.

Makes 6 servings
PREPARATION TIME: 30 minutes
COOKING TIME: 20 minutes plus 30 minutes baking time

Chicken Fried Rice

1½ lb	boneless chicken breast, cut in ½-inch/1 cm pieces	750 g
1 tsp	finely chopped fresh ginger (page 46)	5 mL
1½ tsp	sesame oil, divided (page 13)	7 mL
1 tbsp	soy sauce	15 mL
¼ cup	chicken stock	50 mL
¼ cup	oyster sauce	50 mL
2 tbsp	vegetable oil, divided	25 mL
1 cup	chopped green onion	250 mL
1	sweet red pepper, seeded and diced	1
2	eggs, beaten	2
1 cup	frozen peas, defrosted	250 mL
4 cups	cold cooked rice	1 L

1. In a bowl, combine chicken, ginger, ½ tsp/2 mL sesame oil and soy sauce. Marinate for 20 minutes.

2. Meanwhile, in a small bowl, combine remaining 1 tsp/5 mL sesame oil, stock and oyster sauce.

3. Heat wok or a large non-stick skillet on high heat. Add 1 tbsp/ 15 mL vegetable oil. Add marinated chicken and stir-fry until pinkness disappears, about 2 minutes. Remove chicken and reserve.

4. Add remaining 1 tbsp/15 mL oil to pan. Add green onion and red pepper and stir-fry for 1 minute. Add eggs and stir-fry until just cooked.

5. Add peas and rice and stir until heated through, about 3 minutes. Stir in chicken and sauce and combine well.

Makes 5 to 6 servings
PREPARATION TIME: 20 minutes
COOKING TIME: 10 minutes

Cooked Rice

To cook rice, add 1½ cups/ 375 mL uncooked long-grain rice to 4 qt/L boiling water. Cook uncovered, stirring occasionally, for 14 to 16 minutes or until just tender. You should have about 4½ cups/1.125 L cooked rice. Drain and rinse well with cold water (cooked rice should be dry and thoroughly chilled before being added to stir-fries).

Paella

2	Italian sausages (8 oz/250 g total), removed from casings	2
2 tbsp	olive oil	25 mL
1	onion, chopped	1
2	cloves garlic, finely chopped	2
¼ tsp	hot red pepper flakes	1 mL
1½ cups	uncooked long-grain rice	375 mL
1	sweet red pepper, seeded and diced	1
1	sweet yellow pepper, seeded and diced	1
3	plum tomatoes, diced	3
¼ tsp	powdered saffron	1 mL
½ tsp	dried thyme	2 mL
3 cups	chicken stock	750 mL
½ tsp	salt	2 mL
1 lb	shrimp, shelled and deveined	500 g
1 cup	frozen peas, defrosted	250 mL

1. Heat a large skillet on medium-high heat. Add sausage meat and break up. Cook until browned, about 4 minutes. Remove sausage meat and reserve. Pour off any fat and wipe out pan.

2. Heat oil and add onion, garlic and hot pepper flakes. Cook until softened, about 2 minutes. Add rice and cook for 3 minutes.

3. Stir in sweet peppers, tomatoes, saffron, thyme, chicken stock and salt. Bring to a boil. Reduce heat, cover and simmer for 15 minutes until liquid is almost absorbed.

4. Stir in sausage, shrimp and peas. Cover and continue to cook until shrimp are pink and peas are heated through, about 5 minutes.

Makes 6 servings
PREPARATION TIME: 15 minutes
COOKING TIME: 30 minutes

Rice and Bulgur Pilaf

2 tbsp	olive oil	25 mL
2	onions, thinly sliced	2
⅓ cup	pine nuts, pistachios or almonds	75 mL
1 cup	diced sweet potato	250 mL
1½ cups	uncooked long-grain rice	375 mL
½ cup	uncooked bulgur	125 mL
1	bay leaf	1
2	whole cloves	2
½ tsp	ground cumin	2 mL
3 cups	chicken stock or water	750 mL
½ tsp	salt	2 mL
2 tbsp	chopped fresh parsley or chives	25 mL

1. Heat oil in a saucepan on medium-high heat. Add onions and cook until golden, about 8 minutes. Stir in pine nuts and sweet potato. Cook for 2 minutes.

2. Add rice, bulgur, bay leaf, cloves, cumin, stock and salt. Bring to a boil. Reduce heat, cover tightly and simmer for 18 to 20 minutes or until grains are tender and liquid is absorbed.

3. Stir in parsley with a fork before serving.

Makes 6 servings
PREPARATION TIME: 5 minutes
COOKING TIME: 30 minutes

Rice and Bulgur

Regular white rice has been milled so that the outer hull, germ and most of the bran have been removed. Brown rice has had the outer hull removed, but most of the bran layer remains. It has a slightly nutty, chewy texture. It is more nutritious than white rice because it is less processed, but it takes longer to cook and is often more expensive.

Bulgur is made from whole wheat kernels that have been parboiled and dried, then cracked into coarse fragments.

Polenta with Corn and Italian Sausage

Polenta

Polenta is a cornmeal dish of Italian origin. It can be cooked from scratch or bought already cooked. Refrigerate storebought, ready-to-use polenta after opening and use before the best-before date. It can be sliced and heated on the grill, in the microwave, on the stove or in the oven. Serve it as a side dish sprinkled with cheese or accompanied by a sauce, or use it as the base for a casserole.

2 tbsp	olive oil	25 mL
12 oz	Italian sausage, cut in ½-inch/1 cm pieces	375 g
2	onions, diced	2
2	cloves garlic, finely chopped	2
1	28-oz/796 mL can plum tomatoes with juices, chopped	1
1	sweet red pepper, seeded and diced	1
1 cup	corn niblets, fresh (page 34) or frozen and defrosted	250 mL
1 tbsp	chopped fresh rosemary (or ½ tsp/2 mL dried)	15 mL
½ tsp	salt	2 mL
¼ tsp	pepper	1 mL
1 lb	prepared polenta, cut in ½-inch/1 cm slices	500 g
1 cup	grated mozzarella or Fontina cheese	250 mL

1. In a large skillet, heat oil over medium heat. Add sausage and cook, stirring, until pinkness disappears, about 4 minutes. Add onions and garlic and cook for 3 minutes until softened.

2. Add tomatoes and red pepper. Bring to a boil on high heat. Reduce heat to medium-high and cook until sauce thickens, about 8 minutes. Stir in corn, rosemary, salt and pepper.

3. Meanwhile, arrange polenta slices in a single layer in a lightly oiled 13 x 9-inch/3.5 L baking dish.

4. Spoon sausage and tomato mixture over polenta. Sprinkle with cheese. Bake in a preheated 400°F/200°C oven for 15 minutes.

Makes 6 to 7 servings
PREPARATION TIME: 30 minutes
COOKING TIME: 10 minutes plus 15 minutes baking time

Breakfasts, Lunches and Light Meals

Apple French Toast

Cornmeal Blueberry Pancakes
with Maple Yogurt Sauce

Chocolate Chip Banana Muffins

Ham and Cheese Flan

Sweet Onion and Corn Frittata

Smoked Salmon and Chèvre Bagels

Tex-Mex Salsa Bagels

Bresaola and Cheese Quesadillas

Greek Salad Pitas

Chicken Salad with Mango Chutney Sauce

Shrimp Cocktail Wraps

Grilled Sausage and Onions on Italian Buns

Capicollo, Artichoke and Arugula Focaccia

Chicken Burgers with Baba Ghanouj

Apple French Toast

6 tbsp	butter, divided	90 mL
4	apples, peeled, cored and sliced	4
⅓ cup	granulated sugar	75 mL
½ tsp	ground cinnamon	2 mL
1 tsp	vanilla extract	5 mL
6	slices egg bread, 1¼ inch/3 cm thick	6
3	eggs	3
1¼ cups	milk	300 mL
	Maple syrup or fresh fruit	

1. Melt 3 tbsp/45 mL butter in a skillet on medium-high heat. Add apples and cook for 6 minutes, stirring occasionally, until starting to soften. Sprinkle sugar over apples. Continue cooking for 4 to 6 minutes until apples are tender. Remove from heat. Stir in cinnamon and vanilla. Remove from pan and cool apples to warm or room temperature.

2. Make a pocket in each slice of bread, being careful not to slice all the way through. Divide apple mixture evenly and fill pockets.

3. Beat eggs in a flat dish and stir in milk.

4. Heat remaining 3 tbsp/45 mL butter in a large non-stick skillet on medium-high heat.

5. Dip filled bread slices in egg mixture. Place in skillet. Cook for 4 minutes per side or until golden, adding more butter if necessary.

6. To serve, cut each bread slice in half and serve hot with maple syrup or fresh fruit.

Makes 6 servings
PREPARATION TIME: 15 minutes
COOKING TIME: 22 minutes

Cornmeal Blueberry Pancakes with Maple Yogurt Sauce

MAPLE YOGURT SAUCE:

1 cup	thick unflavoured yogurt	250 mL
¼ cup	maple syrup	50 mL

PANCAKES:

½ cup	all-purpose flour	125 mL
⅓ cup	whole wheat flour	75 mL
⅓ cup	cornmeal	75 mL
2 tbsp	granulated sugar	25 mL
1 tsp	baking powder	5 mL
¼ tsp	baking soda	1 mL
¼ tsp	salt	1 mL
2	eggs, slightly beaten	2
1½ cups	buttermilk or unflavoured yogurt	375 mL
2 tbsp	butter, melted	25 mL
1 cup	fresh or frozen blueberries	250 mL

Pancake-making Tips

- *All ingredients should be at room temperature.*
- *Do not overmix the batter or the pancakes could be tough (it doesn't matter if there are a few lumps).*
- *Turn the pancakes when bubbles appear on the surface, and the edges look dry.*
- *Do not turn pancakes more than once (they will become tough).*

1. In a small bowl, combine yogurt and maple syrup. Reserve.

2. In a large mixing bowl, combine both flours, cornmeal, sugar, baking powder, baking soda and salt.

3. In another bowl, combine eggs, buttermilk and melted butter.

4. Pour liquid mixture into dry ingredients. Stir just until blended. Quickly fold in blueberries.

5. Heat a large non-stick skillet over medium-high heat. Brush pan with butter or oil. Add batter in large spoonfuls. Cook for 2 minutes per side until cooked through. Serve pancakes with maple yogurt sauce.

Makes 12 to 14 pancakes
PREPARATION TIME: 10 minutes
COOKING TIME: 10 minutes

Chocolate Chip Banana Muffins

2¼ cups	all-purpose flour	550 mL
1 tsp	baking powder	5 mL
½ tsp	baking soda	2 mL
pinch	salt	pinch
2	eggs, lightly beaten	2
2	ripe bananas, mashed (about ¾ cup/175 mL)	2
½ cup	granulated sugar	125 mL
⅓ cup	butter, melted	75 mL
1 cup	buttermilk or unflavoured yogurt	250 mL
1 cup	chocolate chips	250 mL

1. In a mixing bowl, combine flour, baking powder, baking soda and salt.

2. In a large mixing bowl, combine eggs, bananas, sugar, melted butter and buttermilk. Mix well.

3. Stir dry ingredients and chocolate chips into egg mixture and combine until just blended. Do not overmix.

4. Spoon batter into 12 large buttered or paper-lined muffin pans. Bake in a preheated 375°F/190°C oven for 20 to 25 minutes or until a cake tester inserted in the centre of a muffin comes out clean and muffins are lightly browned. Remove and cool on wire rack.

Makes 12 large muffins
PREPARATION TIME: 8 minutes
COOKING TIME: 25 minutes

Ham and Cheese Flan

2 tbsp	butter	25 mL
½ cup	chopped onions	125 mL
½ cup	thinly sliced button mushrooms	125 mL
3	eggs	3
1¼ cups	milk	300 mL
2 tbsp	all-purpose flour	25 mL
¼ tsp	salt	1 mL
¼ tsp	pepper	1 mL
1½ cups	grated Cheddar cheese	375 mL
1 cup	finely diced cooked ham	250 mL
2 tbsp	chopped sun-dried tomatoes (page 20)	25 mL
2 tbsp	chopped fresh parsley	25 mL

Cheddar Cheese

Although Cheddar originally comes from England, excellent varieties are made in Canada. Cheddar ranges in colour from white to orange and in age from mild to extra old — the older the cheese, the more crumbly the texture and sharper the taste (old Cheddar will add more flavour to a recipe than the same amount of mild Cheddar).

1. In a small skillet, heat butter over medium heat. Add onions and mushrooms. Cook for 3 minutes until softened. Remove from heat.

2. In a large mixing bowl, whisk eggs. Stir in milk, flour, salt, pepper, cheese, ham, tomatoes and reserved onion mixture.

3. Pour mixture into a buttered 8-inch/2 L square baking dish. Bake in a preheated 350°F/180°C oven for 40 minutes until centre is set. Let stand for 10 minutes before serving.

Makes 5 to 6 servings
PREPARATION TIME: 15 minutes
COOKING TIME: 40 minutes plus standing time

Sweet Onion and Corn Frittata

2 tbsp	olive oil	25 mL
1 cup	diced sweet onion (e.g. Vidalia or Spanish)	250 mL
1½ cups	corn niblets, fresh (page 34) or frozen and defrosted	375 mL
3	green onions, chopped	3
5	eggs	5
⅓ cup	water	75 mL
½ tsp	salt	2 mL
¼ tsp	pepper	1 mL
1 cup	grated Cheddar cheese	250 mL
2 tbsp	chopped fresh parsley	25 mL

1. In a 10-inch/25 cm non-stick ovenproof skillet, heat oil over medium-high heat. Add onion. Cook for 3 minutes until softened. Add corn and green onions. Cook for 4 minutes.

2. In a bowl, beat eggs until blended. Add water, salt, pepper, cheese, parsley and onion/corn mixture. Combine.

3. Return mixture to skillet. Cook for 4 minutes, then place in a preheated 375°F/190°C oven. Bake for 18 minutes until centre is set.

4. Remove frittata from oven, remembering to use a pot holder on the handle. Loosen edges and shake pan. Slide frittata onto serving plate. Serve hot, warm or cold.

Makes 4 to 6 servings
PREPARATION TIME: 10 minutes
COOKING TIME: 30 minutes

Smoked Salmon and Chèvre Bagels

4 oz	cream cheese, at room temperature	125 g
4 oz	goat cheese (chèvre)	125 g
2 tbsp	chopped fresh dill	25 mL
2 tbsp	chopped fresh chives	25 mL
2 tsp	chopped capers	10 mL
1 tsp	honey Dijon mustard	5 mL
	Pepper to taste	
4	bagels	4
4 oz	smoked salmon, sliced	125 g
	Lettuce leaves	

Dill

The popular pickle herb, dill has a slight anise taste. Use it fresh in potato salads, cucumber salads, marinades and with eggs, fish and chicken. The aromatic, feathery leaves and yellow flowers make a flavourful and colourful garnish.

1. In a mixing bowl, blend together cream cheese and goat cheese. Stir in dill, chives, capers, mustard and pepper.

2. Cut bagels in half. Assemble sandwiches by spreading bagels with cheese mixture and topping with lettuce and smoked salmon.

Makes 4 large sandwiches or 8 open-faced sandwiches
PREPARATION TIME:10 minutes

Tex-Mex Salsa Bagels

6 oz	cream cheese, at room temperature	175 g
¼ cup	chopped fresh cilantro (page 39)	50 mL
2	green onions, chopped	2
3	bagels	3
1½ cups	salsa	375 mL
1 cup	grated Monterey Jack cheese	250 mL
½ cup	chopped sweet red or green pepper	125 mL
¼ cup	chopped black or green olives	50 mL

1. In a small bowl, blend together cream cheese, cilantro and onions.

2. Cut bagels in half. Spread cheese mixture over bagels.

3. Place bagels on a baking sheet. Bake in a preheated 350°F/180°C oven for 5 to 8 minutes until warmed.

4. Place bagels on serving plates. Top each with salsa, cheese, sweet peppers and olives.

Makes 6 pieces
PREPARATION TIME: 12 minutes
COOKING TIME: 8 minutes

Bresaola and Cheese Quesadillas

6	10-inch/25 cm flour tortillas	6
⅓ cup	storebought or homemade basil pesto	75 mL
4 oz	bresaola or prosciutto, thinly sliced	125 g
6 oz	provolone cheese, thinly sliced	175 g

1. Place 3 tortillas on a flat surface. Spread with pesto. Arrange bresaola slices over pesto. Top with cheese slices. Place remaining tortillas over cheese.

2. Arrange quesadillas on parchment-lined baking sheets. Bake in a preheated 400°F/200°C oven for 8 to 10 minutes or until light golden.

3. Cool slightly. Cut each into 8 to 12 wedges. Serve warm.

Makes 24 to 36 pieces
PREPARATION TIME: 5 minutes
COOKING TIME: 10 minutes

Provolone

Provolone is a hard cheese from Italy. It is moulded into various shapes and hung to cure. It can be cured for three to twelve months — young provolone has a delicate, smooth taste; aged versions are sharper with a slightly stringy texture. Provolone is an excellent dessert cheese; it grates well and is good in sauces.

Greek Salad Pitas

¾ cup	thick unflavoured yogurt	175 mL
¼ cup	chopped fresh dill	50 mL
¼ cup	chopped fresh mint	50 mL
1 tbsp	lemon juice	15 mL
¼ tsp	salt	1 mL
¼ tsp	pepper	1 mL
1	sweet red pepper, seeded and diced	1
2 cups	seeded and diced cucumber	500 mL
½ cup	diced red onion	125 mL
¼ cup	halved and pitted black olives	50 mL
1¼ cups	crumbled feta cheese (6 oz/175 g)	300 mL
3 to 4	pitas, halved and split	3 to 4

1. In a small bowl, mix together yogurt, dill, mint, lemon juice, salt and pepper.

2. In a large mixing bowl, combine red pepper, cucumber, onion, olives and feta. Add dressing and toss.

3. Spoon salad into pita halves. Serve immediately.

Makes 6 to 8 sandwiches
PREPARATION TIME: 15 minutes

Cucumbers

English cucumbers are available year round and do not need to be peeled. Look for firm ends and an unbruised, dark-green surface. Although English cucumbers do not need to be seeded, some cooks prefer it. Simply halve the cucumber lengthwise and scoop out the seeds with a spoon.

Chicken Salad with Mango Chutney Sauce

MANGO CHUTNEY SAUCE:

½ cup	mayonnaise	125 mL
½ cup	unflavoured yogurt	125 mL
½ cup	mango chutney	125 mL
1½ tsp	curry powder	7 mL
¼ tsp	salt	1 mL

8 oz	snow peas, trimmed (2½ cups/625 mL)	250 g
3 cups	diced cooked chicken	750 mL
1½ cups	thinly sliced celery	375 mL
⅓ cup	pine nuts or slivered almonds, toasted (page 27)	75 mL
1	head Boston lettuce	1
1½ cups	cherry tomatoes	375 mL
	Paprika	

Cooked Chicken

If a recipe calls for cooked chicken, bake four 6-oz/175 g boneless single chicken breasts in a preheated 350°F/180°C oven for 25 minutes. Chill, then dice (1½ lb/750 g raw chicken will yield about 3 cups/750 mL diced cooked chicken). You can also use leftover or storebought barbecued chicken.

1. In a food processor or blender, combine mayonnaise, yogurt, chutney, curry powder and salt. Blend until smooth.

2. Bring a saucepan of water to a boil. Add snowpeas and cook for 30 seconds. Drain well.

3. In a large bowl, combine snowpeas, chicken, celery and pine nuts. Toss. Add dressing and toss to combine.

4. Arrange lettuce leaves on individual serving dishes or platter. Spoon salad over leaves. Garnish with cherry tomatoes and sprinkle with paprika.

Makes 4 to 6 servings
PREPARATION TIME: 20 minutes

Shrimp Cocktail Wraps

½ cup	chili sauce or ketchup	125 mL
1 tbsp	horseradish	15 mL
1 tsp	lemon juice	5 mL
¼ tsp	hot red pepper sauce	1 mL
¼ tsp	pepper	1 mL
¼ tsp	salt	1 mL
3	green onions, chopped	3
12 oz	cooked shrimp, diced	375 g
1	avocado, peeled and diced	1
6	10-inch/25 cm flour tortillas	6
1½ cups	alfalfa sprouts	375 mL
1 cup	grated cucumber	250 mL
1 cup	grated carrot	250 mL

1. In a mixing bowl, combine chili sauce, horseradish, lemon juice, hot pepper sauce, pepper and salt. Stir in green onions, shrimp and avocado.

2. Lay tortillas on a flat surface. Arrange sprouts, cucumber and carrot on bottom third of each tortilla, leaving a border. Divide shrimp filling evenly over vegetables.

3. To wrap, fold bottom over filling, fold in sides and roll up tightly. Cut each roll in half and serve immediately or wrap in plastic and refrigerate for 1 hour. To refrigerate longer, omit avocado and replace with more shrimp or vegetables.

Makes 6 servings
PREPARATION TIME: 25 minutes

Avocadoes

Test an avocado for ripeness by squeezing the fruit carefully — it should yield slightly to gentle pressure. Unripe avocadoes will ripen if they are left at room temperature for a few days. Once they are ripe, store them in the refrigerator, but bring to room temperature before serving.

To dice an avocado, cut it in half and remove the pit. Holding the avocado in the palm of your hand, carefully slice through to the skin, first lengthwise and then across. Gently scoop out the cubes with a spoon.

Grilled Sausage and Onions on Italian Buns

2 tbsp	olive oil	25 mL
3	large onions, thinly sliced (4 cups/1 L)	3
1 tbsp	chopped fresh rosemary (or ½ tsp/2 mL dried)	15 mL
¼ tsp	salt	1 mL
¼ tsp	pepper	1 mL
4	sweet or hot Italian sausages	4
4	Italian buns	4
2 tbsp	coarse-grain mustard	25 mL
2	sweet red or yellow peppers, roasted (page 108) and cut in strips	2
½	bunch arugula (page 19) or watercress (optional)	½

1. In a large skillet, heat oil over medium-high heat. Add onions and cook for 12 minutes until softened and starting to brown. Stir in rosemary, salt and pepper. Set aside and cool to room temperature.

2. Pierce sausages and cook in a skillet, grill pan or on a barbecue over medium heat, turning occasionally, for 15 to 18 minutes or until cooked through. Pour off any fat.

3. Split rolls in half lengthwise. Spread with mustard. Fill rolls with onions, sausages, roasted peppers and arugula.

Makes 4 large sandwiches
PREPARATION TIME: 15 minutes
COOKING TIME: 30 minutes

Capicollo, Artichoke and Arugula Focaccia

1	10-inch/25 cm rosemary focaccia	1
1 cup	grated Gruyère cheese	250 mL
4 oz	thinly sliced capicollo	125 g
1	6-oz/170 mL jar marinated artichoke hearts, drained and chopped	1
12	arugula leaves (page 19)	12
1 tbsp	olive oil	15 mL

Focaccia

Focaccia is a flat yeast bread made from a pizzalike dough and often flavoured with herbs and/or cheese. It can be used in sandwiches, as a pizza base, or warmed and cut into wedges to be served with salad or soup instead of bread.

1. Slice focaccia in half horizontally.

2. Sprinkle half of cheese over bottom half of focaccia. Spread with capicollo, artichokes, arugula and remaining cheese. Cover with top of focaccia. Brush focaccia lightly with olive oil.

3. Wrap focaccia completely in foil. Bake in a preheated 350°F/180°C oven for 20 to 25 minutes or until heated through. (Alternatively, bake on a preheated barbecue over medium heat for 20 minutes, turning 2 or 3 times.)

4. To serve, unwrap and cut in wedges.

Makes 6 to 8 pieces
PREPARATION TIME: 10 minutes
COOKING TIME: 25 minutes

Photo (opposite): Capicollo, Artichoke and Arugula Focaccia (see recipe this page) and Caesar Corn Salad with Chèvre Crostini (see page 20)

Photo (overleaf): Smoked Salmon and Chèvre Bagels (see recipe page 89)

Chicken Burgers with Baba Ghanouj

1 lb	lean ground chicken	500 g
¾ cup	fresh breadcrumbs	175 mL
1	egg	1
3	green onions, chopped	3
¼ cup	chopped fresh mint	50 mL
1	clove garlic, minced	1
¼ tsp	ground cumin	1 mL
¼ tsp	dried oregano	1 mL
¼ tsp	salt	1 mL
4	onion buns	4
½ cup	storebought or homemade baba ghanouj	125 mL
	Watercress, tomato slices and cucumber slices	

Baba Ghanouj

Baba ghanouj is a rich Middle Eastern eggplant puree usually flavoured with garlic, lemon and sesame. Use it as a dip, a spread, or whisk it into salad dressings.

1. In a large bowl, combine chicken, breadcrumbs, egg, green onions, mint, garlic, cumin, oregano and salt. Combine well and form into 4 burgers.

2. Cook burgers on a preheated barbecue, grill or non-stick pan for 8 minutes per side until cooked through.

3. Place burgers on buns. Spread with baba ghanouj and top with watercress, tomatoes and cucumber.

Makes 4 servings
PREPARATION TIME: 15 minutes
COOKING TIME: 16 minutes

Photo (overleaf): Lemon Ricotta Strawberry Shortcake (see recipe page 116)

Photo (opposite): Banana Cake with Chocolate Cream Cheese Icing (see recipe page 117)

Menus

Mother's Day Breakfast in Bed

Orange Sections Sprinkled
with Fresh Mint

Apple French Toast
(page 84)

Quick Children's Dinner

Stir-fried Chicken with Peanut
Sauce (page 36)

Cooked Rice

Fresh Fruit

Spring Brunch

Springtime Asparagus
(page 100)

Chicken Salad with Mango
Chutney Sauce (page 93)

Capicollo, Artichoke and
Arugula Focaccia (page 96)

Fruit and Cheese Platter
(page 123)

Vegetables

Springtime Asparagus

Broccoli and Mushrooms with Oyster Sauce

Braised Artichokes and Potatoes

Southwestern Pepper and Corn Sauté

Baked Eggplant with Tomato Sauce

Spinach with Chickpeas

Fennel with Parmesan

Mushrooms with Corn

Grilled Peppers with Fresh Herb Sauce

Creamy Mashed Potatoes

Tomato Provençal Bake

Butternut Squash and Parsnip Mash

Zucchini with Tomato and Oregano

Roasted Sweet Potatoes, Onions and Cauliflower

Springtime Asparagus

2 tbsp	butter	25 mL
1	small onion, chopped	1
2	carrots, peeled and chopped	2
1 lb	asparagus, trimmed and cut in 1-inch/2.5 cm pieces	500 g
½ cup	water	125 mL
4 oz	snow peas, trimmed	125 g
1	bunch arugula, coarsely chopped (page 19)	1
2 tbsp	chopped fresh chives or green onions	25 mL
2 tbsp	chopped fresh mint	25 mL
¼ tsp	salt	1 mL
¼ tsp	pepper	1 mL

Asparagus

Look for spears with compact, firm, pointed tips and straight stalks. To prepare asparagus, wash it well (especially the tips) and break off the tough base of each stem. If the stems are thick-skinned, peel a few inches up from the base.

Do not overcook asparagus. Steam or boil only until it is tender but still crisp. Plunge the spears into cold water to stop the cooking and pat dry.

1. Heat butter in a large skillet over medium heat. Add onion and carrots and cook until softened but not coloured, about 3 minutes. Add asparagus and water. Cover and cook for 4 minutes or until tender-crisp.

2. Increase heat to high. Add snow peas and cook, uncovered, for 2 minutes to evaporate liquid and cook peas. Add arugula, chives and mint and cook for 1 minute. Season with salt and pepper.

Makes 6 servings
PREPARATION TIME: 15 minutes
COOKING TIME: 10 minutes

Broccoli and Mushrooms with Oyster Sauce

1½ lb	broccoli	750 g
1 cup	chicken stock	250 mL
¼ cup	oyster sauce	50 mL
2 tbsp	soy sauce	25 mL
2 tbsp	cornstarch	25 mL
1 tsp	granulated sugar	5 mL
½ tsp	sesame oil (page 13)	2 mL
2 tbsp	vegetable oil	25 mL
2	cloves garlic, finely chopped	2
1 tbsp	finely chopped fresh ginger (page 46)	15 mL
¼ tsp	hot red pepper flakes (optional)	1 mL
8 oz	button mushrooms, sliced	250 g

Woks

A wok transmits heat evenly and constantly and is ideal for stir-fried dishes that should be cooked for a short time at high heat. If you don't have a wok, use a heavy, deep, preferably non-stick skillet.

1. Trim about ½ inch/1 cm from tough broccoli base and discard. Peel stems and cut into ¼-inch/5 mm diagonal slices. Break florets apart. Steam or blanch broccoli in boiling water until tender-crisp, about 3 minutes. Cool in cold water, drain very well and pat dry.

2. In a small bowl, combine stock, oyster sauce, soy sauce, cornstarch, sugar and sesame oil.

3. In a wok or non-stick skillet, heat oil on high heat. Add garlic, ginger, hot pepper flakes and mushrooms. Stir-fry until mushrooms are just softened, about 2 minutes.

4. Add broccoli and stir-fry for 3 to 4 minutes until heated through.

5. Make a well at base of wok. Stir up sauce and add to wok. Cook for 2 minutes until thickened, stirring constantly. Combine all ingredients well, turn into a serving dish and serve immediately.

Makes 6 servings
PREPARATION TIME: 10 minutes
COOKING TIME: 10 minutes

Braised Artichokes and Potatoes

1	lemon	1
6	large fresh artichokes	6
3 tbsp	olive oil, divided	45 mL
2	onions, thinly sliced	2
4	medium potatoes (1½ lb/750 g), peeled and cut in 1-inch/2.5 cm pieces	4
1½ cups	chicken stock or vegetable stock	375 mL
3	sprigs fresh thyme (or ½ tsp/2 mL dried)	3
½ tsp	pepper	2 mL
½ tsp	salt	2 mL
1 tbsp	lemon juice	15 mL
2 tbsp	shredded fresh basil	25 mL

1. To prepare artichokes, squeeze lemon juice into a large bowl of cold water.

2. Break off outer artichoke leaves until inner yellow ones show. Using a paring knife, shave off tough leaf parts remaining. Trim off bottom stems. Cut 1 inch/2.5 cm from tops of artichokes. Cut each in quarters and remove chokes. Cut each quarter into 2 pieces and place in lemon water.

3. In a large heavy skillet, heat 2 tbsp/25 mL oil over medium-high heat. Add onions and cook until light golden, about 8 minutes.

4. Drain artichokes and add to pan along with potatoes, stock, thyme, pepper and salt. Bring to a boil, reduce heat, cover and simmer for 20 to 25 minutes or until vegetables are just tender. Remove to serving dish and top with lemon juice, remaining 1 tbsp/15 mL oil and basil. Serve hot or warm.

Makes 6 servings
PREPARATION TIME: 18 minutes
COOKING TIME: 35 minutes

Artichokes

Artichokes are the buds of a variety of thistle, and most of the North American supply is grown in California. They are low in calories and high in fibre and vitamin C. You eat the fleshy bases of the leaves as well as the tender hearts, or bottoms.

To prepare artichokes, trim the stems and scrape or pull off the tough outer leaves. Cut off the top third of the artichoke and scrape or pull out the bristly, inedible choke to reveal the heart beneath. The artichokes are cooked when a leaf pulls off easily.

Artichoke hearts are also available in jars or cans packed in brine or oil. Drain them before using.

Southwestern Pepper and Corn Sauté

2 tbsp	olive oil	25 mL
1	onion, chopped	1
2	sweet red peppers, seeded and diced	2
1	jalapeño pepper, seeded and diced	1
½ tsp	ground cumin	2 mL
½ tsp	dried oregano	2 mL
5 cups	corn niblets, fresh (page 34) or frozen and defrosted	1.25 L
2	green onions, chopped	2
¼ cup	chopped fresh cilantro (page 39)	50 mL
¼ tsp	salt	1 mL
¼ tsp	pepper	1 mL

1. In a large skillet, heat oil over medium heat. Add onion and cook until softened, about 2 minutes. Add sweet peppers, jalapeño, cumin and oregano and cook for 2 minutes.

2. Stir in corn. Cover and cook for 3 minutes until corn is just tender. Stir in green onions and cilantro. Season with salt and pepper.

Makes 6 servings
PREPARATION TIME: 12 minutes
COOKING TIME: 8 minutes

Baked Eggplant
with Tomato Sauce

TOMATO SAUCE:

2 tbsp	olive oil	25 mL
2	onions, chopped	2
3	cloves garlic, finely chopped	3
¼ tsp	hot red pepper flakes	1 mL
1	28-oz/796 mL can plum tomatoes, with juices	1
1 tsp	dried thyme	5 mL
1 tsp	salt	5 mL
½ tsp	pepper	2 mL

2 lb	eggplant, cut in ¼-inch/5 mm slices	1 kg
2 tbsp	olive oil (or more)	25 mL
1 cup	fresh basil leaves	250 mL
½ cup	grated Gruyère cheese	125 mL
½ cup	fresh breadcrumbs	125 mL

1. To prepare tomato sauce, in a saucepan, heat oil over medium heat. Add onions, garlic and hot pepper flakes and cook for 3 to 4 minutes or until softened.

2. Break up tomatoes and add to saucepan along with thyme, salt and pepper. Bring to a boil. Reduce heat and cook over medium heat for 25 minutes until thickened. Puree sauce in a food processor or blender.

3. Meanwhile, place eggplant slices on a baking sheet and brush with oil. Cook under a preheated broiler until golden and soft, about 6 to 8 minutes per side. (This may need to be done in batches.)

4. Lightly oil a shallow 13 x 9-inch inch/3.5 L baking dish. Spoon a layer of tomato sauce in bottom. Alternate layers of eggplant, basil leaves and tomato sauce, ending with tomato sauce.

5. In a small bowl, combine cheese and breadcrumbs. Sprinkle over surface.

6. Bake in a preheated 375°F/190°C oven for 30 minutes until bubbling and topping is crisp. Let stand for 10 minutes before serving. Serve hot, warm or at room temperature.

Makes 6 to 8 servings
PREPARATION TIME: 25 minutes
COOKING TIME: 25 minutes for sauce; 35 minutes for final baking

Spinach with Chickpeas

2 tbsp	olive oil	25 mL
2	cloves garlic, finely chopped	2
¼ tsp	hot red pepper flakes	1 mL
1	19-oz/540 mL can chickpeas, drained and rinsed	1
2 tbsp	chopped sun-dried tomatoes (page 20)	25 mL
1 lb	spinach, Swiss chard or rapini, trimmed, washed and coarsely chopped (8 cups/2 L)	500 g
¼ tsp	salt	1 mL
¼ tsp	pepper	1 mL
1 tbsp	lemon juice	15 mL

1. In a large skillet, heat oil over medium-high heat. Add garlic, hot pepper flakes, chickpeas and tomatoes. Cook, stirring, for 2 to 3 minutes or until garlic is fragrant and chickpeas are heated through.

2. Add spinach to skillet. Cover and cook for 3 minutes until spinach has just wilted. Season with salt and pepper. Continue cooking, uncovered, until moisture has evaporated. Just before serving, add lemon juice. Serve hot or at room temperature.

Makes 4 to 6 servings
PREPARATION TIME: 8 minutes
COOKING TIME: 10 minutes

Fennel with Parmesan

4 lb	fennel (3 large bulbs)	2 kg
2 tbsp	olive oil	25 mL
½ tsp	salt	2 mL
¼ tsp	pepper	1 mL
½ cup	grated Parmesan cheese	125 mL

1. Bring a large pot of water to a boil. Trim fennel and cut each bulb into 6 wedges through the core. Add fennel to boiling water and cook for 5 minutes. Drain well.

2. Lightly oil a shallow 13 x 9-inch/3.5 L baking dish. Arrange fennel in one layer. Drizzle with olive oil. Sprinkle with salt, pepper and Parmesan.

3. Bake in a preheated 375°F/190°C oven for 20 to 25 minutes or until fennel is tender and cheese is golden. Serve hot or warm.

Makes 6 to 8 servings
PREPARATION TIME: 8 minutes
COOKING TIME: 30 minutes

Fennel

Fennel is a mildly licorice-flavoured green that can be cooked or used raw in salads or fruit trays. It has a texture similar to celery. To prepare it, cut off the base of the bulb as well as the green stalks and dill-like fronds. Remove any tough outer leaves. Cut the bulb lengthwise into halves or quarters or slice thinly. The fronds can be used as a garnish.

Mushrooms with Corn

2 tbsp	olive oil	25 mL
4	shallots, thinly sliced	4
2	cloves garlic, thinly sliced	2
1	sweet red pepper, seeded and diced	1
8 oz	button mushrooms, thinly sliced (3 cups/750 mL)	250 g
8 oz	shiitake mushrooms, stems removed, thinly sliced (2 cups/500 mL)	250 g
1½ cups	corn niblets, fresh (page 34) or frozen and defrosted	375 mL
2 tsp	chopped fresh rosemary (or ¼ tsp/1 mL dried)	10 mL
¼ tsp	salt	1 mL
¼ tsp	pepper	1 mL

1. In a large skillet, heat oil over medium-high heat. Add shallots, garlic and red pepper. Cook until vegetables are softened, about 3 minutes.

2. Increase heat to high. Add both kinds of mushrooms and cook quickly, stirring, until just softened, about 4 minutes. Stir in corn and continue to cook for 3 minutes. Stir in rosemary, salt and pepper.

Makes 6 servings
PREPARATION TIME: 12 minutes
COOKING TIME: 10 minutes

Grilled Peppers with Fresh Herb Sauce

8	sweet peppers (mixture of red, yellow, orange and green)	8
FRESH HERB SAUCE:		
2	cloves garlic, peeled	2
1 cup	firmly packed fresh parsley	250 mL
½ cup	firmly packed fresh cilantro (page 39)	125 mL
1 tbsp	fresh oregano	15 mL
1 tbsp	fresh rosemary	15 mL
½ tsp	pepper	2 mL
¼ tsp	hot red pepper flakes	1 mL
¼ tsp	salt	1 mL
¼ cup	red wine vinegar	50 mL
¼ cup	olive oil	50 mL

Sweet Peppers

Red and yellow bell peppers are sweeter than green peppers and retain most of their vibrant colour when cooked. Look for peppers that are square in shape (they are easier to core and slice). Remove the cores, seeds and ribs before slicing.

1. Using either a barbecue or broiler, cook peppers on all sides until blackened. Remove and let cool for 20 to 30 minutes. Peel peppers. Remove seeds and cut peppers into strips.

2. Meanwhile, to prepare herb sauce, place garlic, parsley, cilantro, oregano and rosemary in a food processor. Chop finely. Add pepper, hot pepper flakes, salt, vinegar and oil and blend until smooth.

3. In a bowl, combine pepper strips with sauce. Serve at room temperature as part of an antipasto tray or as a side dish.

Makes 4 to 6 servings

PREPARATION TIME: 5 minutes for sauce; 30 minutes to roast and prepare peppers (peppers can be prepared up to 1 day in advance; refrigerate if not using within 2 hours)

Creamy Mashed Potatoes

2½ lb	potatoes (baking or Yukon gold), peeled and quartered	1.25 kg
2 tbsp	butter	25 mL
¾ cup	milk or sour cream	175 mL
4 oz	Brie cheese, rind removed, diced	125 g
3	green onions, chopped	3
1 tbsp	chopped fresh tarragon (or 1 tsp/5 mL dried)	15 mL
¼ tsp	salt	1 mL
¼ tsp	pepper	1 mL

1. Place potatoes in large saucepan. Cover with water. Bring to a boil. Reduce heat and cook for 20 to 25 minutes or until tender. Drain.

2. Meanwhile, in a small saucepan, heat butter, milk and Brie on low heat until just warm.

3. Mash potatoes. Add warmed milk mixture, green onions, tarragon, salt and pepper.

Makes 6 servings
PREPARATION TIME: 10 minutes
COOKING TIME: 25 minutes

Potatoes

Potatoes should be stored in a cool, dark, airy place, but they should not be refrigerated. Remove any sprouted ends and discard any potatoes that have a greenish tinge or green spots. Use larger, floury potatoes (such as baking potatoes or Yukon Gold) in casseroles or baked dishes. Use small new potatoes in dishes like salads, where you want the potatoes to retain a firm texture.

To boil larger potatoes, peel if desired, cut into pieces and cover with plenty of cold water. Bring to a boil and cook until tender. Tiny new potatoes do not need to be peeled. Drop them into boiling water and cook just until tender.

Tomato Provençal Bake

4 tbsp	olive oil, divided	50 mL
6	firm medium tomatoes, seeded and halved crosswise	6
½ cup	fresh breadcrumbs	125 mL
2	cloves garlic, minced	2
¼ cup	chopped fresh parsley	50 mL
¼ cup	shredded fresh basil	50 mL
¼ cup	grated Parmesan cheese	50 mL
½ cup	crumbled goat cheese (optional)	125 mL
¼ cup	chopped black olives (optional)	50 mL
½ tsp	salt	2 mL
¼ tsp	pepper	1 mL

1. In a large non-stick skillet, heat 2 tbsp/25 mL oil over medium-high heat. Place tomatoes cut side down and cook in batches for 6 to 8 minutes or until they start to colour. Carefully turn tomatoes over and transfer to a lightly oiled 11 x 7-inch/2 L baking dish.

2. In a small bowl, combine remaining 2 tbsp/25 mL oil, bread-crumbs, garlic, parsley, basil, Parmesan, goat cheese, olives, salt and pepper. Spread mixture evenly over tomatoes.

3. Bake in a preheated 375°F/190°C oven for 25 to 30 minutes or until topping is golden-brown. Serve hot or at room temperature.

Makes 6 servings
PREPARATION TIME: 6 minutes
COOKING TIME: 40 minutes

Butternut Squash and Parsnip Mash

1	large butternut squash (1½ lb/750 g), peeled, seeded and cut in ½-inch/1 cm pieces	1
4	medium parsnips (1½ lb/750 g), peeled and cut in ½-inch/1 cm pieces	4
¼ cup	milk or reserved cooking liquid	50 mL
2 tbsp	olive oil	25 mL
2 tbsp	finely chopped fresh ginger (page 46)	25 mL
½ tsp	curry powder	2 mL
¼ tsp	ground cumin	1 mL
¾ tsp	salt	4 mL
¼ tsp	pepper	1 mL

Parsnips

Parsnips should be firm and not too wide (specimens with wide bottoms can be woody). Peel them with a vegetable peeler. They can be roasted, mashed or used in soups.

1. Add squash to a large saucepan of boiling water and cook for 15 minutes. Add parsnips and cook for 10 minutes longer until both vegetables are tender. Drain vegetables (reserving ¼ cup/ 50 mL cooking liquid if using). Mash well, adding milk or reserved liquid.

2. Meanwhile, in a small skillet, heat oil over medium heat. Add ginger and cook for 2 minutes until very soft. Add curry powder and cumin and cook for 30 seconds. Remove from heat.

3. Add ginger mixture to vegetables along with salt and pepper. Stir well to combine.

Makes 6 servings
PREPARATION TIME: 15 minutes
COOKING TIME: 30 minutes

Zucchini with Tomato and Oregano

Fresh Tomatoes

Good fresh tomatoes can be hard to find out of season, so good-quality cherry tomatoes and plum tomatoes are sometimes better choices if a recipe calls for fresh tomatoes. Plum tomatoes are meatier and have fewer seeds than beefsteak varieties and are good in salads, sauces or even sandwiches, since they don't ooze their juices as easily.

To seed fresh tomatoes, cut them in half crosswise and gently squeeze out the seeds.

2 tbsp	olive oil	25 mL
2	onions, thinly sliced	2
2	cloves garlic, finely chopped	2
3	medium zucchini (1 lb/500 g), sliced	3
2 cups	chopped fresh tomatoes	500 mL
2 tsp	chopped fresh oregano (or ½ tsp/2 mL dried)	10 mL
½ tsp	salt	2 mL
¼ tsp	pepper	1 mL
2 tbsp	chopped fresh parsley	25 mL

1. In a large skillet, heat oil over medium-high heat. Add onions and garlic and cook for 4 minutes. Add zucchini and cook for 5 minutes. Stir occasionally.

2. Increase heat to high. Add tomatoes, oregano, salt and pepper and cook, uncovered, for 8 minutes until thickened. Stir frequently.

3. Stir in parsley before serving.

Makes 6 servings
PREPARATION TIME: 10 minutes
COOKING TIME: 20 minutes

Roasted Sweet Potatoes, Onions and Cauliflower

3	sweet potatoes (2 lb/1 kg), peeled and cut in 1½-inch/4 cm pieces	3
2	large sweet onions (e.g., Vidalia or Spanish), peeled and cut in 1½-inch/4 cm pieces	2
1	small head cauliflower, broken into florets	1
10	cloves garlic, peeled	10
2 tbsp	chopped fresh rosemary (or ½ tsp/2 mL dried)	25 mL
½ tsp	salt	2 mL
¼ tsp	pepper	1 mL
2 tbsp	olive oil	25 mL

Parchment Paper

Parchment paper, sometimes called baking paper, resists grease and moisture. It is used to line baking dishes, cookie sheets and cake pans to prevent sticking.

1. Place potatoes, onions, cauliflower, garlic, rosemary, salt, pepper and oil in a large mixing bowl. Toss well to coat vegetables with oil.

2. Spread vegetables on a parchment-lined baking sheet. Roast in a preheated 425°F/220°C oven for 45 minutes until tender. Stir a few times during roasting.

Makes 6 servings
PREPARATION TIME: 10 minutes
COOKING TIME: 45 minutes

Menus

Make-ahead Dinner

Chicken and Black Bean Chili
(page 39)

Caesar Corn Salad
with Chèvre Crostini
(page 20)

Banana Cake with Chocolate
Cream Cheese Icing
(page 117)

Winter Buffet

Shepherd's Pie with Sweet
Potatoes and Corn
(page 44)

Green Salad

Fennel with Parmesan
(page 106)

Harvest Streusel Berry Pie
(page 121)

Desserts

Lemon Ricotta Strawberry Shortcake

Banana Cake with Chocolate Cream Cheese Icing

Blueberry Lemon Coffee Cake

Vanilla Cheesecake with Fresh Fruit

Triple Chocolate Chip Cookies

Harvest Streusel Berry Pie

Chocolate Raspberry Trifle

Fruit and Cheese Platter

Lemon Ricotta Strawberry Shortcake

Strawberries

Strawberries do not continue to ripen after they have been picked. Wash the berries quickly under cold water and pat dry gently. Discard any green berries and cut off any bruised parts. Do not remove the hulls and stems until after washing to prevent the berries from becoming waterlogged.

8 cups	sliced fresh strawberries	2 L
¼ cup	orange juice	50 mL
2 tbsp	granulated sugar	25 mL
1½ cups	ricotta cheese	375 mL
½ cup	unflavoured yogurt	125 mL
¼ cup	liquid honey or granulated sugar	50 mL
2 tbsp	lemon juice	25 mL
2 tsp	grated lemon rind	10 mL
1	prepared shortcake flan (6 oz/169 g)	1
	Fresh mint leaves	

1. Place strawberries in a large bowl. Sprinkle with orange juice and sugar. Combine gently. Let stand while preparing filling.

2. In a mixing bowl, combine ricotta, yogurt, honey, lemon juice and rind. Blend well. Refrigerate if not using immediately.

3. To serve, spread ricotta filling over flan. Cut into 8 servings and arrange on serving plates. Spoon strawberries over flan. Garnish with fresh mint leaves.

Makes 8 servings
PREPARATION TIME: 20 minutes

Banana Cake with Chocolate Cream Cheese Icing

2 cups	all-purpose flour	500 mL
1 tsp	baking powder	5 mL
½ tsp	baking soda	2 mL
¼ tsp	powdered ginger	1 mL
¼ tsp	salt	1 mL
½ cup	butter, at room temperature	125 mL
1 cup	granulated sugar	250 mL
2	eggs	2
½ cup	sour cream, unflavoured yogurt or buttermilk	125 mL
3	ripe bananas, mashed (1¼ cups/300 mL)	3

CHOCOLATE CREAM CHEESE ICING:

4 oz	cream cheese, at room temperature	125 g
¼ cup	butter, at room temperature	50 mL
⅓ cup	cocoa powder, sifted	75 mL
1 cup	icing sugar, sifted	250 mL
2 tbsp	cream or milk (or more)	25 mL

1. In a bowl, combine flour, baking powder, baking soda, ginger and salt.

2. In a large mixing bowl, blend together butter and sugar until light. Beat in eggs, sour cream and bananas.

3. Add dry ingredients to banana mixture and stir just until dry ingredients are incorporated. Pour batter into a buttered and parchment-lined 9-inch/23 cm square baking pan. Bake in a preheated 350°F/180°C oven for 35 minutes until a cake tester comes out clean. Let cake cool before icing.

4. To prepare icing, blend cream cheese and butter until very soft. Gradually beat in cocoa and icing sugar until smooth. Beat in cream. If icing is too stiff to spread, add a little more cream. Spread icing over cooled cake.

Makes 12 to 16 servings
PREPARATION TIME: 30 minutes
COOKING TIME: 35 minutes

Blueberry Lemon Coffee Cake

1½ cups	all-purpose flour	375 mL
¼ cup	cornmeal	50 mL
1½ tsp	baking powder	7 mL
½ tsp	ground cinnamon	2 mL
½ tsp	salt	2 mL
½ cup	butter, at room temperature	125 mL
¾ cup	granulated sugar	175 mL
2	eggs	2
1 tbsp	lemon juice	15 mL
1 tbsp	grated lemon rind	15 mL
½ cup	unflavoured yogurt	125 mL
¾ cup	fresh or frozen blueberries	175 mL

LEMON GLAZE:

⅓ cup	icing sugar, sifted	75 mL
4 tsp	lemon juice	20 mL

Blueberries

Since blueberries turn blue long before they are ripe, do not use colour to judge ripeness. To prepare them, pick out any small green berries or stems and rinse quickly under cold running water. Most of the flavour is in the skin, so a handful of small berries can be more flavourful than a handful of large ones. Blueberries freeze well. If you are using them in baking, add them to the recipe in their frozen state.

1. In a medium bowl, combine flour, cornmeal, baking powder, cinnamon and salt. Blend together well.

2. In a large mixing bowl, blend together butter and sugar until light. Beat in eggs, lemon juice and rind.

3. Reserve 1 tbsp/15 mL dry mixture. Add remaining dry ingredients to egg mixture alternately with yogurt and combine well.

4. In a small bowl, toss blueberries with reserved flour mixture. Fold into batter.

5. Spoon batter into a well-buttered 8-cup/2 L tube pan. Bake in a preheated 350°F/180°C oven for 40 to 45 minutes or until a cake tester comes out clean. Cool in pan for 10 minutes, then turn out.

6. To prepare glaze, in a small bowl, combine icing sugar and lemon juice. Brush over top and sides of cake while it is cooling. When cake is cool, wrap well in plastic.

Makes 8 to 10 servings
PREPARATION TIME: 25 minutes
COOKING TIME: 45 minutes

Vanilla Cheesecake with Fresh Fruit

1½ cups	chocolate cookie crumbs	375 mL
½ tsp	ground cinnamon	2 mL
⅓ cup	butter, melted	75 mL
1 lb	cream cheese, at room temperature	500 g
½ cup	granulated sugar	125 mL
2	eggs	2
1 tbsp	all-purpose flour	15 mL
2 tsp	vanilla extract	10 mL

TOPPING:

1 cup	sour cream	250 mL
2 tbsp	brown sugar	25 mL
1 tsp	vanilla extract	5 mL
4 to 5 cups	fresh fruit (e.g., sliced strawberries, raspberries, diced pineapple, sliced peaches)	1 to 1.25 L

Raspberries

Fresh raspberries are very fragile and perishable. Use them as soon as possible after buying and wash them quickly and gently, if at all.

1. In a bowl, combine cookie crumbs with cinnamon and melted butter. Pat into bottom and part way up sides of a 9 inch/23 cm springform pan. Chill while preparing filling.

2. In a large bowl, blend together cream cheese and sugar until very light. Add eggs, flour and vanilla and beat until just blended.

3. Pour batter over crust. Bake in a preheated 325°F/160°C oven for 35 minutes until just set.

4. To prepare topping, in a small bowl, combine sour cream, brown sugar and vanilla. Spread over cheesecake. Return to oven and bake for 5 minutes. Chill completely.

5. To serve, carefully remove outside rim of pan. Cut cake into slices and serve with fresh fruit.

Makes 10 to 12 servings
PREPARATION TIME: 25 minutes
COOKING TIME: 40 minutes

Triple Chocolate Chip Cookies

1 cup	butter, at room temperature	250 mL
¾ cup	packed brown sugar	175 mL
½ cup	granulated sugar	125 mL
2	eggs	2
1 tsp	vanilla extract	5 mL
2⅓ cups	all-purpose flour	575 mL
1¼ tsp	baking soda	6 mL
¼ tsp	salt	1 mL
1 cup	white chocolate chips	250 mL
1 cup	milk chocolate chips	250 mL
1 cup	semisweet chocolate chips	250 mL

Chocolate

Many different kinds of chocolate can be used in baking. Semisweet chocolate is slightly sweeter than bittersweet. White chocolate is very sweet and consists of sweetened cocoa butter mixed with milk solids and sometimes added vanilla. All three make good eating chocolate. Unsweetened chocolate is used in baking recipes where the sugar is added separately.

1. In a large mixing bowl, blend together butter and both sugars until very light. Beat in eggs one at a time. Add vanilla and blend in.

2. In a separate bowl, mix together flour, baking soda and salt. Add to creamed mixture until just blended. Stir in three kinds of chips.

3. Drop batter by tablespoonful onto an oiled or parchment-lined baking sheet.

4. Bake in a preheated 375°F/190°C oven for 8 to 10 minutes or until golden. Cool slightly. Remove from baking sheet and cool on a wire rack.

Makes about 60 cookies
PREPARATION TIME: 15 minutes
COOKING TIME: 10 minutes per baking sheet

Harvest Streusel Berry Pie

2 cups	raspberries, fresh or frozen	500 mL
1 cup	blueberries, fresh or frozen	250 mL
1 cup	quartered strawberries, fresh or frozen	250 mL
1/3 cup	granulated sugar	75 mL
3 tbsp	quick-cooking tapioca	45 mL
1	9-inch/23 cm deep pie shell	1
1/3 cup	all-purpose flour	75 mL
1/3 cup	rolled oats	75 mL
1/3 cup	brown sugar	75 mL
1 tsp	ground cinnamon	5 mL
1/3 cup	butter, cold	75 mL

1. In a large bowl, combine raspberries, blueberries and strawberries.

2. In a small bowl, blend together granulated sugar and tapioca. Stir into berries and combine well. Pour into prepared pie shell.

3. Place pie on a foil-lined baking sheet. Bake in a preheated 400°F/200°C oven for 15 minutes. Reduce heat to 350°F/180°C and continue to bake for 20 minutes before adding topping.

4. Meanwhile, in a mixing bowl, combine flour, rolled oats, brown sugar and cinnamon. Cut in butter until it is in tiny bits.

5. Sprinkle pie with streusel topping. Return pie to oven and bake for an additional 20 to 25 minutes or until filling is bubbling and top is golden. Cool on a wire rack.

Makes 6 to 8 servings
PREPARATION TIME: 15 minutes
COOKING TIME: 60 minutes

Chocolate Raspberry Trifle

¼ cup	cornstarch	50 mL
½ cup	granulated sugar	125 mL
2 tbsp	cocoa powder, sifted	25 mL
¼ tsp	salt	1 mL
2 cups	milk, divided	500 mL
1 cup	cream	250 mL
2	egg yolks	2
6 oz	semisweet chocolate, finely chopped	175 g
2 tbsp	dark rum or brandy	25 mL
8 oz	prepared angel cake, broken in 1-inch/2.5 cm pieces (4 cups/1 L)	250 g
4 oz	white chocolate, chopped	125 g
2 cups	fresh raspberries	500 mL
1 cup	whipping cream	250 mL
	Raspberries and fresh mint leaves	

Fresh Nuts

Store nuts in a well-sealed container in a cool, dark, dry place (or freeze them if you are not using them right away), as fresh nuts go rancid quickly; 1 lb/ 500 g nuts in the shell will yield about 8 oz/250 g shelled nuts. To remove the inner skins from freshly shelled almonds, place them in a sieve and pour boiling water over them — the skins should slip off.

1. To make filling, in a heavy saucepan, combine cornstarch, sugar, cocoa, salt and ½ cup/125 mL milk. Stir well until smooth. Stir in remaining 1½ cups/375 mL milk and cream. Place over medium heat. Cook, stirring constantly, for 5 to 7 minutes or until thickened.

2. In a bowl, beat egg yolks. Add 1 cup/250 mL hot milk mixture to yolks, then return to saucepan. Cook for 2 minutes, stirring constantly. Remove from heat.

3. Add chocolate and rum to saucepan. Stir until chocolate melts. Pour mixture into a clean bowl. Cover with plastic wrap and cool to room temperature.

4. In a large serving bowl, alternate layers of filling, cake, white chocolate and raspberries, beginning and ending with filling. Cover and refrigerate for 3 hours.

5. To serve, whip cream and pipe onto trifle in rosettes. Garnish with raspberries and mint leaves.

Makes 10 servings
PREPARATION TIME: 20 minutes
COOKING TIME: 15 minutes plus refrigeration time

Fruit and Cheese Platter

6 oz	dried figs and/or dates	175 g
½ cup	apricot nectar	125 mL
¼ cup	water	50 mL
½ tsp	anise seeds	2 mL
6 oz	dried apricots	175 g
¾ cup	apple juice	175 mL
1 tsp	vanilla extract	5 mL
4 oz	Montasio cheese	125 g
4 oz	Stilton cheese	125 g
4 oz	shelled fresh almonds	125 g
4 oz	shelled fresh walnuts	125 g
10	slices Panettone	10
10	slices Melba toast	10
2	oranges or clementines, peeled and separated in sections	2

1. In a saucepan, combine figs, apricot nectar, water and anise seeds. Bring to a boil. Boil for 3 minutes. Turn off heat. Cover and cool to room temperature.

2. In another saucepan, combine apricots, apple juice and vanilla. Bring to a boil. Boil for 4 minutes. Turn off heat. Cover and cool to room temperature.

3. On a large serving platter, arrange figs/dates, apricots, cheeses, almonds and walnuts. Arrange Panettone, Melba toast and orange sections among cheese, nuts and fruit.

Makes 8 to 12 servings
PREPARATION TIME: 15 minutes
COOKING TIME: 10 minutes plus cooling time

Montasio Cheese

Montasio is a skim-milk cow's cheese from the Veneto region of Italy. It is a dense cheese with a smooth yellow rind and tastes similar to Asiago. A young Montasio makes an excellent eating cheese; aged varieties are usually grated and used in cooking.

Stilton Cheese

Stilton is a creamy, blue-veined mould cheese from Britain. It has a crumbly texture and a wrinkled rind. It is milder, smoother and less salty than other blue cheeses.

Index